Creativity in Literacy

Ceri Shahrokhshahi

Acknowledgements

I would like to thank the following people in Nottingham for their contributions, support and patience in the making of this book – Carmen Joseph, Angela O'Dea and the children in 1J, Kayla Green, Kate Randall, Alex Broughton and Rachael Sharpe and, most of all, Carol Smiths-Adam, head teacher Linda Claxton and my lovely children in 6S 2006–7 at Sycamore Junior School in St Ann's; Chris Castleton and the staff at Sycamore Infants; Jane Cash and the staff and children of Horsendale Primary School; Mark Scotton and the staff and children of Annie Holgate Junior School in Hucknall, Nottingham and Melanie Pemberton at Portland Primary School, Bilborough. A special thanks to artist Jed Brignal and the head teacher Wayne Norrie and children of Rufford Junior School.

The publishers would also like to thank Tranmoor Primary School and Church Vale Primary School for their artwork.

I would like to dedicate this book to my father, Tony Boundy, whose teaching, philosophy and wisdom will remain with me always and to my husband, Farnoosh, and my children, Laila and Aria, who make my world go round!

Characters from stories by Eric Carle (pages 28–29)

Commissioning Editor: Zoë Nichols   Editor: Joanne Mitchell   Cover design: Steve West
Page layout: Barbara Linton   Photography: Roger Brown

p35 (bottom left): Display supplied by teachers and children. The image is in no way an actual representation of the FAIRTRADE Mark.

First published in 2008 by Belair Publications.

Every effort has been made to trace the copyright holders of material used in this publication. If any copyright holder has been overlooked, we should be pleased to make the necessary arrangements.

British Library Cataloguing in Publication Data. A catalogue record for this publication is available from the British Library.

ISBN 9781 84191 459 6

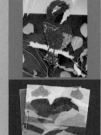

Contents

Introduction

For many years, the teaching of literacy has been relegated to a rigid one hour a day. It is now recognised that many of the skills and concepts taught within the subject link successfully to other subjects in a thematic and creative manner. *Creativity in Literacy* is not just about linking artwork to a piece of text, it is about finding natural links between Literacy, Numeracy, Science and so on, in order to deepen a child's understanding and enjoyment of that text or skill. *Creativity in Literacy* is about engaging children in the learning process in a dynamic and creative way. Each theme has a variety of suggestions for text (and, in some cases, Internet sites) to use as scaffolding, linking different subject areas and activities to the text.

The 17 themes cover a range of texts and are suitable across the primary age range. They offer opportunities for teachers to link their own ideas and differentiated activities with the suggestions. They seek to promote creativity in thinking, approach and in written work. The artwork and displays have been produced by children for children.

Literacy Tips

- Make a story sack for each text that is studied. Place items linked to the text into the bag. Second-hand shops sell all sorts of toys, books and character dolls that can be placed in the bag. Get pictures of the characters and create key words. Laminate these and place them in the bag ready to stimulate discussion or to use as a prompt during written work. Story sacks work for all ages!

- Record the text and have a copy available with a listening laboratory and headphones in the classroom. Children can reinforce their understanding of the text and enhance their listening and reading skills by working independently at the listening station.

- Collect a selection of DVDs linked to the text. Watch these with the children and while they are watching, ask them to jot down thoughts and images on individual whiteboards or 'stick-it' labels. These form a good vocabulary bank for literacy work. It also 'hooks' reluctant writers into the task.

- Have the children draw characters from the text. Use the images to recreate the text and ask the children to scribe their version of the story.

- Suspend a large sheet of bubble wrap across your quiet area. When children have completed a piece of written work, pin it to the bubble wrap. It extends your display space and is an immediate record of the children's work.

- Connect the class computer to a website on the Internet that is relevant to the text so that children can work independently as an extension or for research purposes prior to or during written work.

Art and Display Tips

- Contact a local card or paper manufacturer. Very often they will let you have their off-cuts for free.

- Always have play dough available in plastic bags. Keep it in the fridge.

- Salt dough is a great modelling substance and is cheaper than clay. It can be baked in an oven or microwaved.

- Use PVA glue and water to varnish models.

- Collect shoeboxes from shops. They make great 'setting bases' for themed work and for recreating the scenes in a story.

- Use double-sided tape to stick objects together as it's easier than sellotape.

- Use the inside of cereal boxes as card – it's good quality and you're helping to save the planet.

- Use Velcro to attach labels for interactive displays in the classroom.

Classroom Organisation

- Identify areas in your classroom for workstations. Link these with the core subjects, or to a thematic unit. Have everything needed for independent or extension work in plastic tubs with handles (this reduces clutter).

- Buy a listening laboratory with headphones. They encourage reluctant readers, and are ideal for large classes when you need a group of four to six children to work on their own for extended periods of time. Have multiple copies of books available and record the text beforehand, so they can listen and read.

- Convert large cereal boxes into storage containers by cutting diagonally from the rim to about three-quarters of the way up. Cover with wrapping paper. Each child can have one of these with their name on it to store workbooks, reading books and writing equipment.

- Have a quiet area in the classroom with large cushions. This can be used by individuals or groups of children for reading and other activities. It is also ideal for children on the autistic spectrum, as it gives them a space for a time out.

- Create a 'worry box' out of a shoebox. Children can place their worries in it on small pieces of paper. You can read these and work with the children to sort out their worries or use examples as generic ideas during discussion time.

In writing this book, I have drawn ideas from experienced staff, suggestions from children and tried and trusted strategies I have employed in my classroom. I hope they will be of use to you as either a starting point for extended work or stand-alone activities that encourage the use of literacy as a springboard for a creative curriculum.

Ceri Shahrokhshahi

Animal Fun

Resources

- *Handa's Surprise* by Eileen Browne (Walker Books Ltd)
- *Oi! Get Off Our Train* by John Burningham (Red Fox)
- *The Tiger Who Came to Tea* by Judith Kerr (Collins Picture Lions)
- *Dear Zoo* by Rod Campbell (Campbell Books)
- CD: *The Carnival of the Animals* by Saint-Saëns
- www.nationalgeographic.com
- www.panda.org
- http://pbskids.org/backyardjungle/

Starting Points

- Read *Handa's Surprise* by Eileen Browne. Discuss what happens in the story and ask the children to write about a day in the life of a child in an African country.
- Write a poem based on the animals in the story, such as a giraffe. This could be displayed on a template of the animal with legs made from folded card.

- Have a bowl of fruit in the classroom based on the fruit in Handa's basket. Sit the children in a circle and ask a child to pick out a piece of fruit and describe it to the rest of the class. Pass the fruit onto another child who has to think of more words to describe it. Repeat until the children run out of ideas. Change the fruit and repeat the process.

Display

- Make sunset pictures. Wet an A4 sheet of paper and paint horizontal layers onto the sheet using purple, pink and blue watercolour paints. Leave to dry and then, using black paint, draw trees and shrubs. Stick down black silhouettes of animals onto the sheet.
- Create pictures of Handa on black sugar paper. Do the same with African animals such as giraffes, elephants and lions. Ask the children to write down what they think Africa is like for the main character in the story. Type these out. Display the writing, sunset pictures and large pictures of Handa on a display board backed in pink. Complete the display with silhouettes of the animals in the story.

Further Activities

- Hold a class debate. Discuss whether animals should be kept in zoos. Half of the class should generate the pros, and the other half, the cons of zookeeping. Talk about endangered species.

- Read *Oi! Get Off Our Train* by John Burningham. Ask the children to generate questions to ask the animals in the story about their habitats, foods, why they are in danger and how they feel. Split the class into pairs. The first child asks questions and the partner 'hot seats' the role of the animal and gives their personal response. Discuss why these animals are endangered. Record ideas and thoughts on a whiteboard. Use the website www.panda.org to investigate what is being done to help endangered species.

- Write acrostic poems based on animals found in the savannah. Display the poems with the title 'Jungle fun' cut from camouflage wrapping paper. Add animals made from paper with concertina legs. The children could write a description of the animal. Display papier mâché heads of the animals along with photographs of animals in the wild.

- Choose an animal to describe entitled 'What am I?' Ask the children to research five facts about this animal. Type them out. They must not mention the name of the animal. Other children have to use the clues in the writing to name the animal. Draw or print off a picture of the animal and stick it underneath the text. Place a sheet of paper over the picture to hide it. Once the children have guessed the animal correctly they can 'lift the flap' to reveal the animal.

- Ask 'How do animals adapt to life in zoos?' Contact a local zoo to arrange a trip. At the zoo, the children could record details regarding habitat, care and whether the animal is an endangered species.

- The children could put together a jigsaw puzzle of a zoo animal. Use a template of a jigsaw and photocopy onto A3 sheets of paper. Ask the children to draw their animal on the reverse side and colour. Then write a simple set of instructions of how to re-assemble their jigsaw.

Cross-curricular Links

Dance and Drama

- Produce a visual interpretation of the text *Oi! Get Off Our Train* by John Burningham. Ask the children to choose an animal they would like to be and practise how the animal moves – slowly with swinging movements for elephants, stretched up tall and swinging their arms for giraffes, crawling on all fours and growling for lions and so on. Another group can become the train and experiment with movements – place their hands on the waist of the child in front and co-ordinate their movements as they move across the floor. Once the children have their movements organised, play the music from Saint-Saëns *The Carnival of the Animals* and encourage the children to move to the rhythm and the beat of the music.

Art and Design

- Create some camouflage artwork. Using yellow and white, ask the children to mix increasing amounts of either colour to investigate tones of colouring in a giraffe or lion.

- Collage a full-size animal, such as a lion, and place in a camouflaged habitat using a variety of art materials.

Science

- Investigate the habitat of a wild animal. Look at how wild animals are adapted for life in their environment.

- Investigate camouflage as a means of survival. Focus on predator/prey in the wild. Each child studies the camouflage colours of a certain animal (tiger, leopard, giraffe and so on). They copy these patterns using tissue paper or sticky paper and collate them onto sheets of paper. Stick these down onto lift-up flaps. Place a picture and a description of the wild animal underneath the flap as an interactive display. Place a border around the display using an animal's markings, such as a tiger with orange and black markings. Take the shape of an animal, such as a snake, and generate words to describe the textures of the animal's skin and stick these down onto the snake shape.

- Investigate food chains using animal templates. Cut out black templates of the sun, grass and some animals such as an elephant, a giraffe and a rhino. Place them on a 'sunset' background. This can be made by using chalk and dragging the chalk horizontally across the page to form bands of colour. Blend the layers together. Spray with hairspray afterwards to prevent the chalk smudging. Type out key words to describe the food chain – producer (sun), consumer (animal). Place these labels in a raised envelope. Children stick the labels in the correct places on the display.

- Younger children can paint pictures of birds. They then draw a smaller picture to attach to the main painting of an animal that the bird eats such as a snail or a slug. Place a piece of paper over this 'prey'. Use as an interactive food chain activity. What does this animal eat? Open the flap to reveal the snail.

- Using the website http://pbskids.org/backyardjungle/, children explore the 'back yards' of children in the United States. Some of the animals found are imaginary and have descriptions added to them. Others are real and include details of the animals' lifestyle. These can be used as a starting point for creative writing.

Maths

- After reading *The Tiger Who Came to Tea* by Judith Kerr, use the children's ideas for making a meal for the tiger and buy the required ingredients. Look at the imperial and metric weights on each product, for example, butter 250g. Explore ways of sharing these amounts between two, four and five tigers. How much of the ingredients would each tiger need? What would be left over?

Design and Technology

- Read again *The Tiger Who Came to Tea*. In this story, the tiger eats everything in the house. Ask the children which of the foods they like best. Ask them which is their favourite day of the week and what they eat on that day, for example, Friday might be pizza on the menu at school. Discuss what tigers eat. Do they eat the same things in the zoo and in the wild?

- Read *Dear Zoo* by Rod Campbell. Discuss the animals in the story and what they eat. Would they eat the same food that the children eat? Create masks to match the animals in the story. Sit the children in a circle. Whilst wearing their mask, they should describe to the rest of the class what their animal likes to eat and its preferred habitat. These could also be used in the drama activity on the previous page.

- The children could design their favourite meal and an imaginary one for the tiger using salt dough.

Geography

- Using atlases, ask the children to choose an area in the world that they would like to visit or explore. They should decide the reasons why, such as it's hot, they have watched a TV programme about the place and so on. Produce a travel diary by folding A4 sheets of paper in half and stapling in the centre. Set them the task for both homework and school work to find out as much as they can about this area and record it in their diaries using pictures, illustrations and text. Use these diaries as points for discussion in class. The children can produce a PowerPoint presentation or a class 'share and tell' session from the research they have undertaken.

Dinosaurs

Starting Points

- Have a class discussion about dinosaurs. Using a flip chart, ask the children to write down any questions or facts that they know about dinosaurs, such as why they became extinct, what they ate and so on. Use these as a starting point when reading *The DK Big Book of Dinosaurs* by Angela Wilkes. If any questions remain unanswered, use the website www.bbc.co.uk/dinosaurs to find answers to their queries.

- Show the children an excerpt from the Disney film *Dinosaurs*, where the meteorites fall from the sky. Discuss what the dinosaurs saw in this part of the film. What is the atmosphere of this section? How are the animals in the film feeling at this moment? Ask the children to record their thoughts on paper. Discuss 'Is this film fiction or non-fiction?', 'Are dinosaurs fictional?' and 'How do we know they are not?'

Resources

- *The DK Big Book of Dinosaurs* by Angela Wilkes (Dorling Kindersley Publishers Ltd)
- *Dinosaurs and All That Rubbish* by Michael Foreman (Puffin Books)
- *How To Keep Dinosaurs* by Robert Mash (Weidenfeld & Nicolson)
- DVD: *Dinosaurs* (Disney)
- DVD: *Walking With Dinosaurs* (BBC)
- www.bbc.co.uk/dinosaurs
- www.ecover.com/us/en/Contact

Display

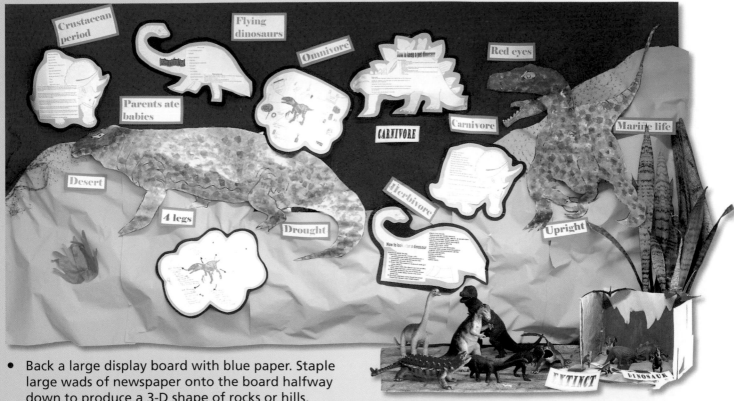

- Back a large display board with blue paper. Staple large wads of newspaper onto the board halfway down to produce a 3-D shape of rocks or hills.

- Produce large replica dinosaurs from card and paint using sponges. Staple these to the display and stuff with newspaper for a 3-D effect.

- Make labels with key words, for example, 'extinct', 'carnivore', 'omnivore', 'flying' and so on. Attach these to the display.

- Place a selection of plastic dinosaurs on the table top so that children can look at them and play with them. Use these as a stimulus for free writing. Take one of the plastic dinosaurs and study it. Ask the children to write about how it moved (on two or four legs), if it just lived on land or if it flew, and which of the other dinosaurs on the table this dinosaur would eat.

- Display a 3-D shoebox environment with smaller dinosaurs on the table top. Discuss the environments that the dinosaurs lived in, such as savannah/shrub land, treetops, nests on the top of mountains and so on.

Further Activities

- Read *Dinosaurs and All That Rubbish* by Michael Foreman. Discuss the key elements of the text – dinosaurs come back to life to save the world; mankind has managed to do harm. What is the resolution to the problem in the text? (The dinosaurs become eco-warriors.) Discuss how to help to heal the planet. Ask the children to write a letter to the local environment agencies asking them what steps they are taking to recycle rubbish and how they encourage people to be more eco-friendly. Write a letter to the 'Ecover' company about their environmental-friendly products or contact them online at www.ecover.com/us/en/Contact.

What you need:
A large skip
Metal large food bowl
Extra large dino pool
Metal padlock mail box
Metal solid gold plated cage
Safe environment
50 tons of bed sheets
Large litter box
Shovel/to pick up dinos mess
Carnivore and herbivore (meat,veg)

First you need a metal secure cage.

Second take the dinosaur for a walk in the park.

Thirdly need to make sure it does not bite.

Fourthly you have to buy their accessories: food, water, bedding.

Fifthly you need to clean their mess up.

- Using the above book as a starting point, talk about the recycling of newspapers, cans, glass bottles and jars, aluminium foil, motor oil and scrap metal. Investigate local recycling centres. Make your school a recycling centre. The children could design a newsletter for parents and the community advertising the fact that your school has become a recycling centre.

- Share the text and illustrations from the book *How To Keep Dinosaurs* by Robert Mash. Discuss with the children how to look after a fictitious 'pet' dinosaur. The children should generate ideas, such as build a large wooden cage, have a large litter tray ready, build a small pool for the dinosaur to play in and so on. List the pet requirements as labels around the picture on the A3 sheet. Illustrate with pictures of the pet equipment.

- Ask the children to create a habitat for a dinosaur and write a short description about it on the board or flip chart. They should tell the class the sort of conditions the dinosaur of this habitat would live in. Make the habitat from a cardboard box or shoebox. Cut the front out, or leave it as a flap. Using newspaper, build up a habitat for the dinosaurs. Make rocks and an uneven surface from paper. Glue over the 3-D padding with tissue or coloured paper. Add water for drinking and trees or shrubs to add impact. Place small model dinosaurs into the habitat. In small groups or pairs, ask the children to use the box scene as a setting stimulus for creative writing. Build up the suspense in a story, for example, 'the large dinosaur prowled amongst the rocks until it spotted a single egg by the side of the pool…'

- Watch extracts from *Walking With Dinosaurs* and focus on the habitats in the programmes. Make notes on a large flip chart to refer to during the follow-up activities. Use plastic dinosaurs to recreate scenes and scenarios using the ideas from the programmes. Extend by children enacting conversations between the dinosaurs and record their dialogue on a tape recorder. Feed the recorded work back to the class for shared ideas of dialogue to develop into a narrative story.

Cross-curricular Links

Maths

- Have a tray of sand in the classroom. Lay a series of string grids across the top of the sand tray and label the grid with co-ordinates. Bury small models of either dinosaurs or bones. In small groups, the children role-play the task of archaeologists discovering the fossils. On pre-prepared sheets with co-ordinate grids printed on them, ask the children to record where they found the remains.

- Stick a series of dinosaur pictures down on a sheet of paper. Ask the children to find out the exact height of the animals. Translate the measurements from metres into centimetres. List any other measurements the class can find – weight, length and so on. Using newspaper, make an outline of one of the dinosaurs in a large open space. Extend to measurements of children. In pairs, measure parts of bodies – from tip of finger to shoulder, neck to waist and so on. Using the recorded measurements, make a newspaper replica on the playground/hall. Compare the children's measurements with those of the dinosaurs.

- Cut out and staple three large overlapping circles (a Venn diagram) to a display board. Print out a selection of carnivorous (meat-eating), omnivorous (meat and vegetable) and herbivorous (vegetarian) dinosaurs and stick on backing paper. Attach Velcro strips to the back of the dinosaurs and the three circles on the display. Ask the children to attach the dinosaurs into the correct section.

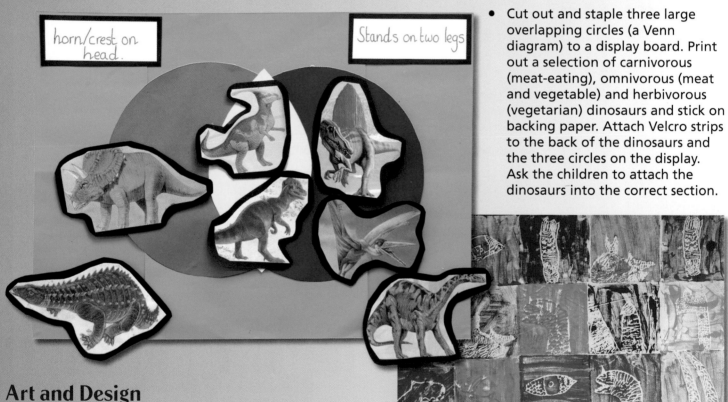

Art and Design

- Ask the children to sketch part of a dinosaur onto paper. They might choose an eye that is lizard-like, the long neck of a brontosaurus, the claws of a meat eater and so on. Transfer the design onto a polystyrene print sheet using a sharp pencil. Apply paint to the print sheet and press it firmly onto a sheet of paper to make a print of the dinosaur. Allow the prints to dry and then attach all the squares together to form a dinosaur banner.

Science

- After reading *Dinosaurs and All That Rubbish*, make a recyclable bottle. Take three large plastic one-litre bottles. Cut the top half off one, then cut the centre of another and the bottom half off the third. Place the middle half into the base and fit the top into the middle. Place vegetable matter into the middle and spray with water. Tape the top of the bottle closed. Leave in a warm place and record how the vegetable matter decays.

- Talk about the habitats around the time of the dinosaurs. Make a salt volcano from a jar, vegetable oil, salt, water and food colouring. Pour three inches of water into the jar. Pour a third of a cup of oil into the jar. Ask the children 'Is the oil on top of the water?' and 'Why?' Add a drop of food colouring to the mixture. What happens? Shake salt on top of the oil. Count to five. Add more salt. At each stage, ask the children to predict what might happen next. How can they illustrate/record this? Children should be guided towards observing shape, colour, sound and movement of the liquids. What changes can they observe? What might have caused these changes?

Design and Technology

- Create a 'designasaurus'. Have a selection of dinosaurs/models/pictures/books/website addresses available for reference. Identify the features of the dinosaurs – upright, small legs, length and so on. As a class, choose a series of features to mesh together into a new dinosaur. Draw this as a class using a flip chart. Put together a history of the dinosaur. Name it. Where was it found? What did it eat? How did it look after its young? How would it move? What was its habitat like? Explore vocabulary and extend to making new words. Develop a class glossary.

- Build the 'designasaurus'. Using cardboard boxes, assemble the base of a dinosaur. Put chicken wire around the boxes and bend into an outline. Make limbs out of coat-hangers. Stuff with newspaper and then papier mâché the model.

Children of Winter

Starting Points

- Tell the following story to the class:
  The Derbyshire village of Eyam – with almost 350 inhabitants before the plague – has achieved particular fame for the tragedy and courage that were seen there. In September 1665, a tailor received a parcel of cloth that was infested with plague-carrying fleas. One by one, the villagers came down with the disease. It might have spread to the rest of the county but for the rector William Mompesson. He persuaded the villagers not to flee, but to stay in self-imposed quarantine until the plague had run its course. They left money soaked in vinegar at a well on the outskirts of the town for food and supplies to be left for them. The plague came to an end in October 1666, with almost three-quarters of the villagers – 259 people from 76 families – dead.

- Read *Children of Winter* by Berlie Doherty, a story about the plague village of Eyam. The story starts in the present, with three children (Catherine, Patsy and Andrew) and their parents setting out for a walk across the Derbyshire moors to visit their grandmother. During a storm the children lose sight of their parents and shelter in an old barn. They are somehow transported back in time to 1665 when the plague spread from London to Eyam. They become their ancestors – Catherine, Tessa and Dan Tebbutt, who were taken to the barn outside of their village to protect them from the plague. Their mother tells them to remain in the barn and not let anyone in until a message comes to tell them it is safe to return home.

Display

- Cover a large display board with black paper. Cut out icicle shapes for the top border. Make a large copy of the plague doctor (who visited the houses of those dying from the disease) and decorate with tissue paper. Display pictures of scenes of life in Eyam during the plague years, such as the villagers leaving the money at the well, the villagers gathering outside for church services and so on, on the board. Label key points of the plague, such as fleas and remedies, and place examples of the children's work next to the labels.

Further Activities

- Have copies of *Children of Winter* available for group reading. Read chapters one and two. Discuss surnames in the class and their history, for example, Smith (ironmongers). Identify where children in the class have been born and if their surnames are common to that area. Using the Internet, research the family trees of children or investigate meanings of surnames.

- Make 'historical' bags. Use these as props to stimulate creative writing. Add artefacts from different time periods, for example, for *Children of Winter* there could be some cloth, a candlestick holder and herbs.

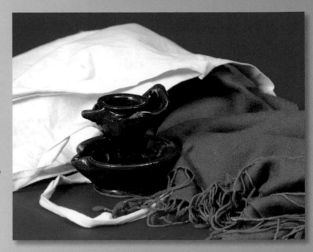

- Write a diary entry. Give each child a scenario, such as, 'You have just been told that a virus has broken out in your school and the head teacher says that you will be in quarantine for three weeks.' They should write about how the news was broken, what the symptoms of the disease are, how they will eat, sleep and keep clean, and how they will communicate with their family. If they are allowed to bring a rucksack, what would they need/bring?

- Read the first chapter of *Children of Winter* again. Concentrate on the sections where Catherine 'pretends'. Read a section of the book that describes an event or a setting. Ask the children to close their eyes. Take them on a journey back through time – choose events in history. Ask the children to imagine they are there and to call out what they see, then what they hear and smell. Write the children's 'images' on a flip chart. When the children open their eyes, share the 'image words' with them. Write a whole class journey back in time using their ideas.

- Investigate the symptoms of the plague. Ask the children to write a description of someone who shows symptoms of the plague. What will happen to them? What do they look like? Invent a cure for the plague – try to make up the strangest cures, for example, in the seventeenth century, people felt that carrying herbs protected them; smoking a pipe would cure it; rubbing mercury onto the body and sitting in a bread oven were all 'cures'. The children could take the role of the plague doctor – ask them what treatments you could use.

- Using some of the medieval and seventeenth-century ideas of how to avoid the plague researched on the Internet, ask the children to create a modern-day poster advertising ways of avoiding the plague.

Cross-curricular Links

History

- Write a report on what is known today about the plague. Use websites such as www.channel4.com/history. Discuss what caused the plague. Some believed it was a punishment from God, others that it was the position of the planets. Construct arguments for and against these beliefs, taking the point of view of how people in the seventeenth century observed the world around them. The children could record findings on paper shaped like rats and mount on black paper. Put all work in a large book. Decorate the cover with straw to resemble thatching and put sticky-back plastic over it.

- Investigate the Great Fire of London. Ask the children to imagine they are visiting the city for the first time. Research what the buildings of London would look like. Ask, 'What would the sounds from the streets be and what did people wear?' and 'What happened when the plague struck?' Put together a pictorial record of these times. Create writing logs that chronicle events of the time.

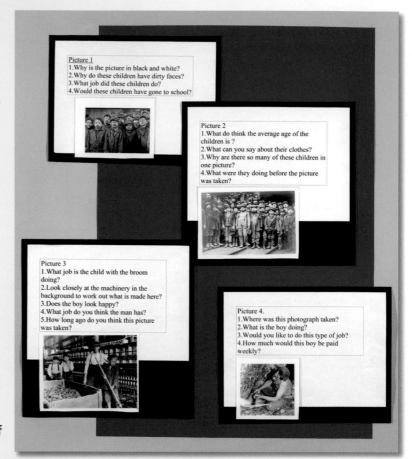

- Discuss the conditions for the people living in the story, *Children of Winter*. Extend this discussion by asking the children to think of other events in history where conditions have been difficult for children. The children could conduct their own research project, for example, the child miners of the early twentieth century. What were the conditions like? Show them relevant pictures. Mount these on card and laminate. Attach question cards to each picture: 'Where would this have been taken?', 'How long did these children have to work each day?', 'How much did they earn?', 'What were the conditions like?' and 'What were their rights?'

Science

- Read the nursery rhyme *Ring a Ring o'Roses*. Discuss the use of herbs in medieval medicine. Grow herbs in a warm place in the class. Include rosemary, basil and so on. Use herbs to make sachets.

- Collect a variety of herb samples to smell and discuss in the classroom. Place the herbs in white bags (without labels) and pass around a circle for the children to smell and guess the herb. Then label the bags accordingly.

- Make herb pillows. Collect lavender and rosemary. Sew a rectangular piece of cloth, leaving one end open. Insert herbs and seal. Place under pillows or in drawers at home. The children could decorate their pillows with sequins or other felt shapes stuck to the pillow.

- Look at the diseases caused by bacteria; use the plague as a starting point. Make a bacteria terrarium. Each child has a container with lid. Place vegetable or fruit matter into it with water and seal the lid. Mould will start to appear in two to three days. The children could draw and comment on the changes as they occur (daily). Look closely at the colours of the mould on the different foods and the changes that take place in the food itself, for example, food gets smaller, dries out and so on.

 Note: Do not open the lid at the end of the experiment! Dispose of the closed, sealed containers in an outside waste disposal facility such as a skip.

Maths

- Re-read chapter one of *Children of Winter* where the children in the story have a rucksack each. Ask the class to investigate designs for rucksacks that will hold their belongings. Make a paper rucksack out of brown sugar paper. Measure the sides of the rucksack using centimetres and millimetres. Cut out the template and assemble using sellotape. Extend by having a competition to see how much the rucksack can hold. Use tins of beans. Ask, 'How can you reinforce the bag to hold two, three and four tins of beans?' and 'What is the maximum weight a rucksack in the class can hold?'

- Photocopy a map of the local area or the village of Eyam in the story onto A3 paper. Draw a co-ordinate grid on top of the map – more able children can use all four quadrants. Identify symbols in each quadrant. Extend by asking children to give co-ordinates of places and things on the map.

- Compare now and then. Discuss how people travelled to school or work then, and how they travel now. Gather data from sources. Make a pie chart, line graph or bar graph to show data.

Design and Technology

- Ask the children to design a rucksack such as the one used in the story *Children of Winter*. Discuss what it might look like. It needs to hold 2kg of weight which is the average weight of a rucksack when going on a short trip. Make the rucksacks from papier mâché or other junk materials.

- In the Middle Ages in Europe, people's diet depended a lot on how wealthy they were. Wealthy people also ate a lot of bread, but they made their bread out of wheat. Using a bread maker, make a selection of breads. Extend by having a selection of breads from around the world – naan, black bread, granary and so on. Ask the children to complete a survey on the country of origin, appearance, colour, shape, texture and flavour of each bread.

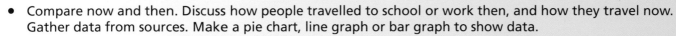

Geography

- Mining was an active industry in the area surrounding Eyam. Investigate mining of lime, slate and fluorspar. What uses do these minerals and rocks have in today's society? Use an area in the school grounds where the children can dig holes. Put samples of soil and rocks found on a tray. How deep can the holes go? Discuss what the children think they might find. Dig up to a safe depth. Take the samples back into class and photograph them. Using computers, children label their samples – black rock, round pebble, brown soil and so on. Using web resources, investigate the different types of rocks they may have unearthed – sedimentary, igneous and so on. Use the website www.kidsgeo.com to investigate the different types of soil and rocks.

Where the Wild Things Are

Resources

- *Where the Wild Things Are* by Maurice Sendak (Red Fox)
- www.animalsonline.com/

Starting Points

- Read *Where the Wild Things Are* by Maurice Sendak. Ask the children what they think of the pictures. Do they bring the text to life? Ask the children to write down their opinions of the story and illustrations on whiteboards. Then share their ideas and opinions with the class.

- Make a wild thing from junk modelling materials and papier mâché. Use these 'wild things' for a speaking and listening activity. Before showing their models, the children should describe to their partner what their wild thing looks like. Their partner then writes about or draws the creature.

- Ask the children to write a story about their wild thing.

Display

- Back and border a display board. Drape material in one corner. Ask the children to make large drawings of the characters in *Where the Wild Things Are* – the monsters, Max, the dog. Decorate and mount with the characters facing Max as though they are having their 'rumpus party'. Label the display 'Where the Wild Things Are!'.

- Add the children's stories to the board once typed up.

Further Activities

- Look at the illustrations from *Where the Wild Things Are*. Ask the children to write down or say five things that the Wild Things have in common, for example, big eyes and sharp claws. Discuss how each Wild Thing is a combination of different creatures, such as the head of an eagle and so on.

- Concertina several pieces of A4 plain paper. Give each child a piece and ask them to draw the head of their 'Wild Thing'. Fold it over so the head is not visible. Pass this to the next child who then draws the top half of the monster. Fold over and pass on until the monster is complete. Open these out to see what their 'Wild Thing' looks like. Children can then describe through writing or speaking what the 'Wild Thing' looks like. Extend by giving it a name and what type of personality it might have. Then write about or draw the creature.

- Take one 'Wild Thing' example from the above activity and display on the whiteboard. Get the children to write on the board any adjectives, verbs, adverbs that they think of when looking at the image. Write out these words and display next to a painted illustration of a Wild Thing as 'Wow Words' for use in future literacy work.

- Divide the class into groups. Give each group a different scene from the story to illustrate on A4 paper with brief text statements underneath. When the groups are finished, have them peg their story parts in order onto a clothes line to create a complete class story.

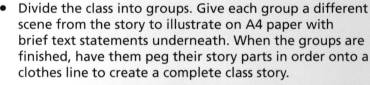

- Use the website www.wildanimalsonline.com to investigate real wild animals and choose one to 'adopt' as a class project.

19

Geography

- Sailors believed that the Earth was flat and that when you reached the end of the Earth there would be monsters or you would fall off. Max sailed across the oceans and found monsters at the end of his journey! Look at a globe and satellite pictures to prove that the Earth is not flat.

- Max sails away from his home in a boat. Research the history of boats and sailing.

- Identify famous mariners, for example, Christopher Columbus and Sir Walter Raleigh, and track one of their journeys. Investigate their reasons for undertaking journeys.

- Look at biographies of famous mariners. Questions could include 'Why did they travel?', 'How did they travel?', 'What dangers lay ahead?' and 'What did they discover?'

Science

- Using the text of *Where the Wild Things Are*, discuss the beginning, the middle and the ending of the story. How many habitats does Max appear in?

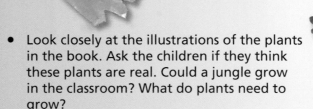

- Look closely at the illustrations of the plants in the book. Ask the children if they think these plants are real. Could a jungle grow in the classroom? What do plants need to grow?

- Have a selection of seeds available for the children to look at. What plants would they grow into? Do big seeds make big plants and so on? Ask the children to draw what they think the seeds might grow into. Ask them to make up 'vegetables' or 'fruit' that might be a combination of several things, for example, a banana and an orange become a 'banorange'.

- Create a mini ocean. Fill a plastic bottle three-quarters full of water. Add blue food colouring and then add cooking oil. Leave about one inch at the top of the bottle. Point out that oil and water do not mix. Tilt the bottle back and forth to see a wave effect.

Design and Technology

- Using K'Nex, Lego or Meccano, ask the children to design their own Wild Thing. It must move in four different ways, balance and be free standing. Once made, the children could record how they made their figure, what problems they encountered and how they were solved.

- Design a boat for Max. Use a range of materials such as plasticine, salt dough, clay, bark and so on. Use a range of designs and shapes – flat, curved, bowl shaped and so on. Have a competition to see which one floats the longest. Discuss reasons. Extend by looking at size, material and shape.

Maths

- Ask the children, 'How many plants could fill our classroom?' Using card, make a 3-D room. Find out the perimeter and the area. Cut out small circles of card like plant pot bases. How many of these would fit in the base of the room?

- Investigate plants that grow tall quite quickly. Plant sunflowers, cress and other fast-growing seeds and keep a record of their measurements on a weekly basis.

Art and Design

- Read *Where the Wild Things Are* to the class. Create a Wild Things area in a corner of the classroom using a variety of art materials. For example, place fishing wire across the 'ceiling' of the room and drape green tissue paper and so on to resemble the trees that grow in Max's room.

- Give each child a large piece of white paper and craypas, crayons, wax crayons. While reading the story, ask the children to draw whatever images come to mind. Lay these down on the floor and write down words – adjectives, nouns, phrases – that describe what they see in the pictures/images.

- Draw a large sailing boat similar to the illustration of Max's boat. Put panels in the boat and make 'doors'. Put examples of writing behind each door, such as the children's version of a page in the book, descriptions of the Wild Things, their party, what they look like, how the children think the Wild Things acted when Max left, illustrations of the Wild Things and Max's room.

- Mix warm water with salt and food colouring. Draw abstract pictures on paper using the solution. When the water evaporates, the salt will leave patterns behind. Use these as backing-paper for the children's Wild Things written work.

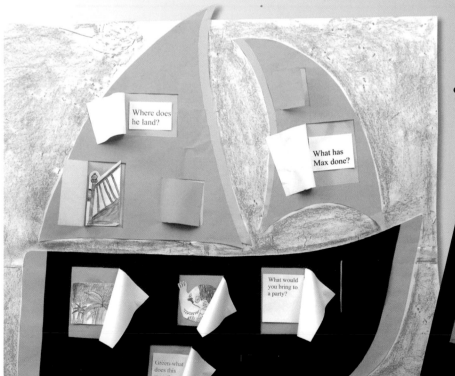

Flour Babies

Starting Points

Resources

- *Flour Babies* by Anne Fine (Puffin Books)
- www.toyrus.com
- www.keepkidshealthy.com

- Read *Flour Babies* by Anne Fine. It is the story of Simon Martin, a boy from a broken home. His class, 4C, are the worst students in the school, and Simon is the worst of all of them. The class is given a science project about parenting. They must look after a bag of flour for three weeks as though the bag was a baby, and write about what happens every day in a 'baby diary'.

- Bring in a packet of flour and explain to the children that they will be looking after the 'flour baby' for a week, taking it in turns. Draw up a rota for looking after the 'baby'. Ask children to volunteer in taking the 'flour baby' home at the end of the school day. Alternatively, each child could bring in a small bag of flour to make individual flour babies. Discuss that the 'flour babies' are to be looked after at all times by the children and treated as though they were real babies. Children may personalise their 'flour babies'. Wrap the flour bag in masking tape and draw a face on a piece of paper to stick on it. Make legs and arms from either card, or stuff tights with newspaper to make arms and legs, and attach to the babies to make them more realistic. Children may like to bring in clothes from home to dress their 'babies'.

- On a flip chart, record the children's ideas and questions for looking after the 'baby'.

- Read the first three chapters of *Flour Babies* by Anne Fine. Focus on the five rules for looking after the flour babies – clean, weighed, in sight at all times, a baby book kept and a Social Services check of the baby. Get an adult to pose as a member of Social Services to come into the class during the first week to do a spot check on how well the children are looking after their flour babies.

- Ask the children to keep a 'baby diary'. On the first page, they should write down what clothing their baby will have and illustrate and explain their choices.

Display

- Back a large display board with paper and place a pink border around it.

- Ask the children to paint their flour babies dressed in clothes. Cut out the flour babies and mount them on card.

- Use one of the flour baby diaries the children have produced and mount on the display board.

- Produce a family tree for a flour baby and display amongst the paintings.

- If possible, use 'baby accessories' below the display such as a crib, magazines, nappies, dummies and so on.

Further Activities

- Discuss the clothing of the flour baby in the story – frock and bonnet. Ask the children what they would dress their flour babies in. They should dress their babies by the next lesson, deciding on gender and age.

- Design a birth certificate for the flour baby based on an actual one.

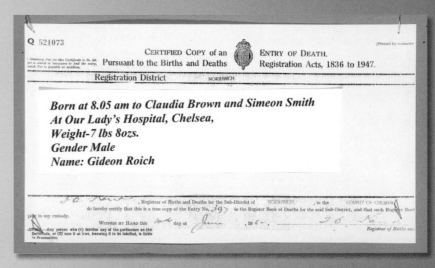

- Discuss with the children how a family can grow and change. For example, a new baby could be born, a grandparent could move in, an older brother or sister could move away to university, or the family could move to another town. Children could offer examples from their own family lives. As a speaking and listening activity, ask the children to interview members of their families and make a list of important events. They could record their family tree/ time lines in chronological order. Ask them to make a record of facts in a flour baby book, as the baby is the newest member of their family.

- Look at the oral tradition of lullabies and nursery rhymes. Read *Rock-a-bye baby* to the children and discuss what they think the storyline is. Use the Internet to find out the origin of the rhyme and choose three other nursery rhymes to investigate together.

- Ask the class how they can get really good at doing something. Write their ideas down in the baby book. Link them with how well they are managing as carers.

- Discuss what it means to be young and old. Ask the children to cut out pictures of older and younger people from magazines. Record their responses to the questions, 'What does it mean to be old?' and 'What does it mean to be young?'

- Look on websites such as www.toysrus.com. Cut and paste items that are needed to look after a newborn baby – pram, cot, nappies and car seat. The children should find the cheapest items online, as well as the most expensive. These could be stuck into the flour baby books.

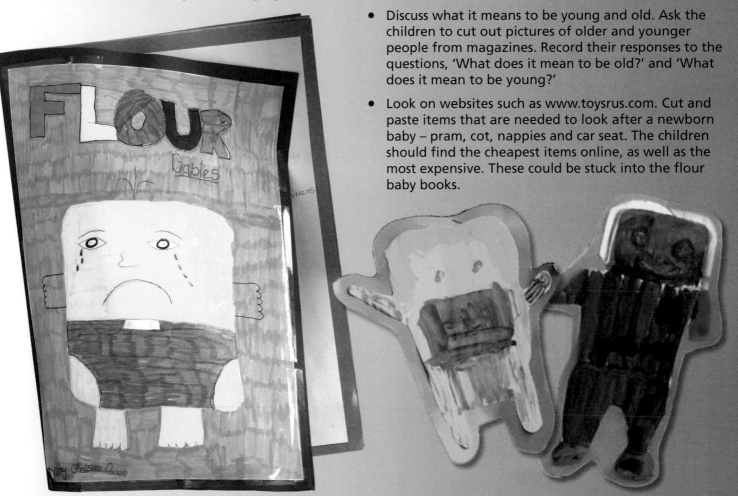

Cross-curricular Links

History

- Set the children the task of finding out the history of the potty. Track the invention back to its earliest roots and compare with the range of potties available for babies these days. Focus on modern-day potties that sing, talk and congratulate the children!

- Show the children a photographic collection from your family stretching back several generations. Discuss with the children who they think the people are (mum, aunty and so on). If possible, also include pictures of babies.

PSHCE

- Discuss families and the links with who we are today. Re-read chapter three of *Flour Babies* and talk about Simon Martin's discussion with his mother about when he was a baby and why there are no photos of his father. Be sensitive to children in the class who have similar family situations. Use this as an opportunity to discuss and celebrate all types of families.

- What rules do children need? Ask the children to think of three different ways of guiding laws and rules that do not use negative words. Think of five rules for the school and class that can be shared in an assembly. Write these on A3 paper stained with tea and singed around the edge with a match to look like parchment.

> **Guiding rules.**
> I will care for others
> I will appreciate my successes
> I will know who I am
> I will aim high
> I will learn from my weaknesses.

Science

- Investigate car seats and booster seats for children. Talk about why children need more protection in cars than adults. Use the Internet to help with research, for example, www.keepkidshealthy.com.

- Discuss what babies eat in their first few months before they go onto baby food. Bring a blender into school and use a range of vegetables and fruit to create baby foods.

Art and Design

- Create a personal museum. Take the inside of a shoebox or cereal box. Cover with coloured paper. Ask the children to bring in objects from their childhood such as photos, toys, materials from clothing and so on. They should stick the objects down inside the box. Experiment with the 3-D space to create a personal Museum of Childhood.

- Make a family tree model. Turn a foam cup, open end down, and secure on a flat surface using masking tape. Cover with green or brown tissue paper, textured to resemble bark. Draw members of the children's family onto card and colour using crayons and felt-tipped pens. Attach each family member to the end of a toothpick and stick into the cup. Make leaves from paper or card and stick into the cup in between the family.

Maths

- Explore the boom of designer items for babies, especially in clothing. Find examples on the Internet. Print and stick down in a baby book. Label each item with the price and the reason the baby would need these items. Ask the children to find alternative items that are not designer and to compare the prices. They could work out how much money is saved by not buying designer items and so on. Make a display from their results using the printed items necessary for the baby for its well-being and health contrasted with items that are not necessary, such as designer shoes and clothing, and the costs saved.

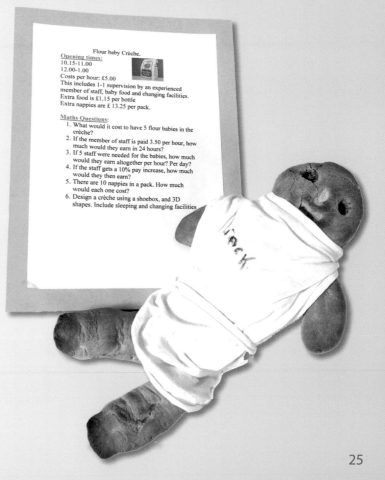

- In chapter five of *Flour Babies*, Sajid describes his scheme of having a private crèche for the flour babies in order to raise money. Give the children an imaginary scenario: There are 15 babies in a crèche; there is one care assistant to every three babies in the crèche. Each care assistant earns £35.00 a day. Each parent must pay £15.00 per day to have their children in the crèche. How much would the owners of the crèche earn in profit each day? (£50.00). Extend by including food, heating and running costs for the crèche on a daily basis. Investigate the costs at a nursery/crèche near you. The children should organise a crèche in the classroom so the flour babies do not get taken out at playtime. Decide pricing, care arrangements and activities.

Flour baby Crèche.

Opening times:
10.15-11.00
12.00-1.00
Costs per hour: £5.00
This includes 1-1 supervision by an experienced member of staff, baby food and changing facilities.
Extra food is £1.15 per bottle
Extra nappies are £ 13.25 per pack.

Maths Questions:
1. What would it cost to have 5 flour babies in the crèche?
2. If the member of staff is paid 3.50 per hour, how much would they earn in 24 hours?
3. If 5 staff were needed for the babies, how much would they earn altogether per hour? Per day?
4. If the staff gets a 10% pay increase, how much would they then earn?
5. There are 10 nappies in a pack. How much would each one cost?
6. Design a crèche using a shoebox, and 3D shapes. Include sleeping and changing facilities.

Favourite Stories

Starting Points

- Read *The Gingerbread Man* and discuss the main character, the gingerbread man. What type of person is he? Is he selfish because he runs away from the people that made him? Why does he run away? What would have happened to him if he had stayed?

- Look at other versions of the story such as *Gingerbread Baby* and compare with the original. Ask the class how they think the old man and the old woman felt about their gingerbread baby running away.

- Compare *The Gingerbread Man* with the story of *Pinocchio* whose father made him because he wanted a child. Each story has a different ending. The gingerbread man gets eaten, and Pinocchio becomes a real boy because he learnt the lesson of love.

- Prepare templates shaped like the gingerbread man. Ask each child to write a new version of the story on the template. Make card covers for the stories and put the templates together as a book. With younger children, ask them to illustrate the story whilst you scribe the text to create a class book.

Display

- Using large sheets of wallpaper backing, draw rough templates in black felt-tipped pen of the main characters from *The Gingerbread Man* and paint them using poster paints. Cut out the figures and attach hair using wool or corrugated card.

- Cut out a winding path from black paper. Place the painted gingerbread man at the beginning of the road. Place characters such as the little boy and girl near the path. Display children's illustrations of the journey on the path. Cut out a blue pond and attach the character of the fox next to it.

- Ask the children to write their own versions of the traditional tale onto A4 sheets of paper. Fold them so they open in the middle like windows. Back these onto a large sheet of paper and attach to the display for the children to read.

- In bold font, type out the key points of the text such as 'Run, run as fast as you can' and attach these to the display.

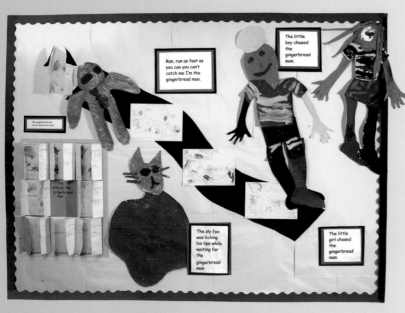

Further Activities

- Use the Internet to find other traditional tales, such as www.nationalgeographic.com/grimm/ which offers interactive fairy tale activities.

- Change the character of the fox in the *The Gingerbread Man* to another animal. Would a cat have eaten the gingerbread man? Look at the role and character of the fox in traditional tales and fables. He is usually wily and sneaky. Why is this the case? Watch *The Fox And The Hound*. Discuss the characters of the fox and the hound in the film. Point out that both characters are expected to behave in a certain way and yet they don't. Ask the children to write down their views about how other characters in the film perceived the main characters and what they were actually like.

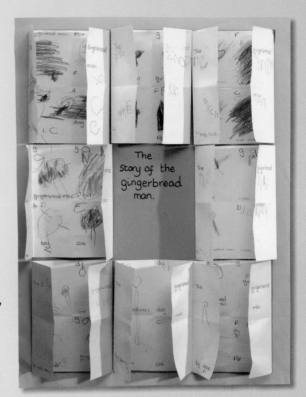

- What might a modern-day gingerbread man look like? Would he react in a different way to his journey? Give the gingerbread man modern cars/speedboats and so on to help him on his journey. Use small model cars and boats to help the children re-enact the journey. Have the children record or write down their new versions of the story. Encourage the use of sounds in their writing, for example, how they think the sound of a speedboat would be written.

- Read other traditional tales, such as *Jack and the Beanstalk.* Ask the children to draw pictures from the story and to add labels. On a large display board, back with yellow and make a beanstalk out of brown paper that forms a semicircle up the sides and across the top. Attach leaves covered in transparent green plastic to the stalk. Display children's drawings and text underneath the stalk.

- Create a story starter sack for a traditional tale, such as *Little Red Riding Hood.* Take a pillowcase and place items into it related to the story, for example, a tape of the story, the story book, a basket, a toy wolf. (Many second-hand shops sell items that are great for story sacks.) Print off character cards, laminate and place in the sack. Pull out any item and discuss with the children where it might fit in the story. Put the characters into order of importance.

27

Cross-curricular Links

PSHCE

- Discuss the rights and wrongs in *Jack and the Beanstalk*. Did Jack ever get told off for stealing? Did the giant deserve his fall? Ask the children to write persuasive texts for and against the issues. Talk about other issues raised in the story, such as taking care of your family, the importance of money, and whether stealing is the right thing to do.

Art

- Choose an author/illustrator whose books are popular in your class. In the example shown, the children chose Eric Carle. Read a selection of stories from the author and then ask the children to recreate the characters in a similar style to the illustrator, using similar art techniques. They could then write about the different characters and this could be added to a class display about the author.

- After reading Jan Brett's *Gingerbread Baby*, have the children brainstorm the items the gingerbread baby will need to live inside the house that was created for him. Cut out a large gingerbread house out of corrugated card. Attach to a wall space within the classroom. Children can work together to cut out and paint different types of sweets to decorate the house. Make a large door that opens and reinforce using masking tape. Create a 'writing and reading' station inside the house. Use the area for independent writing. Have pens, whiteboards or large sheets of paper for children to rewrite the story in their own words. Have books linked with the theme inside for children to take out and read. Have a tape recorder available for children to listen to taped versions of *The Gingerbread Man* and other traditional tales.

- Using a large piece of card or paper, make a child-sized character from a favourite story, for example, *The Gingerbread Man*. Collage using small squares of tissue paper or sponge paint. Write sections of the story around the outside of the shape.

PE

- After reading *Jack and the Beanstalk*, discuss how many different types of 'beans' there are, such as jelly bean, has-been and kidney bean. Play with the words. Can the children translate these phrases into actions, such as string bean – stretch very tall, and kidney bean – curl up? When you call out a type of bean, the children should do the appropriate action.

Maths

- Ask the children to measure parts of their bodies and compare with characters in their favourite stories, such as the giant in *Jack and the Beanstalk*. Use discussion starters such as 'I am 120cm tall, the giant is five times taller than me, how tall is the giant?' and 'My feet are size three, the giant's feet are five times bigger than mine, what shoe size is he?'

- Make the beanstalk in *Jack and the Beanstalk*. Make the stalk out of large tubes and papier mâché onto the 'stalk'. Attach leaves made from cardboard. Place Velcro on each of the leaves. Attach maths questions to each leaf with Velcro. Children should take a question and complete the task.

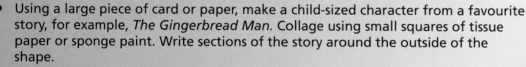

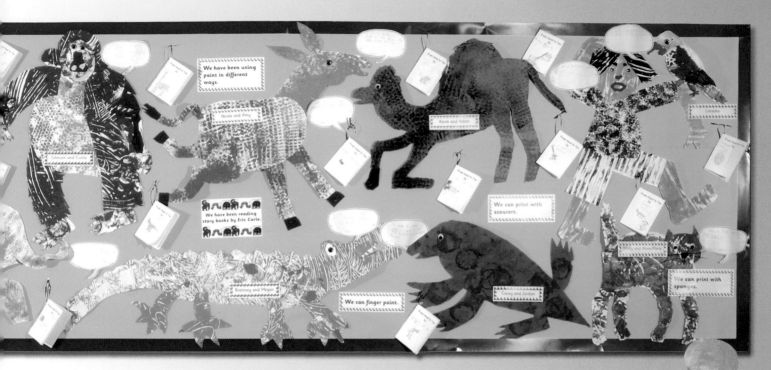

Geography

- On the whiteboard, create a sectioned path showing the journey the gingerbread man took until he was eaten or arrived at the gingerbread house. Ask the children to create a board game to show the journey of the gingerbread man. The object of the game is to get to the house first. Roll the dice, land on sections and draw cards (these can be linked with a maths or literacy activity, for example, 'What is 2 × 3?' or 'How many vowels in a phrase?'). The children can draw along the path to illustrate the journey on the board game path.

Science

- Grow a bean plant indoors in a small sturdy pot. Once it sprouts, insert a six to nine inch thin branch or stick gently in the pot to help the plant climb the branch. Each child should make a small drawing of themselves and tape it to the top of the branch to pretend they are Jack climbing the beanstalk.

Time Travelling

Resources

- *Dr Xargle's Book of Earthlets* by Jeanne Willis and Tony Ross (Andersen Press Ltd)
- *Harry Potter and the Philosopher's Stone* by J.K. Rowling (Bloomsbury)
- *The Monster Bed* by Jeanne Willis and Susan Varley (Andersen Press Ltd)
- DVD: *Dr Who* (2 Entertain Video)
- CD: *Dark Side of the Moon* by Pink Floyd (EMI)
- www.nasa.gov/audience/forkids

Starting Points

- Explore the concept of time-travelling by watching extracts from a *Dr Who* DVD. Create a time-travelling machine in the classroom. Get a very large cardboard box painted to look like the Tardis (telephone box). Get each child to pretend they have gone into a time-travelling machine and ended up in the past. As a speaking and listening exercise, discuss what they would see and who they would meet. Record initial thoughts onto a large sheet of paper in the shape of the Tardis.

- Ask the children to research some events in history and to choose key characters, times and incidents and use these as a scaffold for narrative writing about time travelling.

Display

- Create a time tunnel in a shared area of your school, such as the library. Using masking tape, attach large cardboard tubes to walls at equal distances along a corridor or in an area of the classroom. Place large branches of trees or willow twigs into the tubes and attach to the ceiling to form a series of interlocking arches. Thread basket weaving cane between the arched twigs to form a canopy. Keep doing this and experiment with shapes such as ovals, circles and spirals. Wrap masking tape around two strands of twig or basket weaving to form a flat surface.

- Paste PVA glue onto masking tape. Stick tissue paper onto the glue. Paste and repeat the process. Attach bits of jewellery, fabric, plastic flowers and photos to the decorated area with a glue gun and build up a tunnel or cave. In the example shown, each class should choose how to decorate the area outside their classroom.

Further Activities

- Read *Dr Xargle's Book of Earthlets* by Jeanne Willis and Tony Ross. Display the picture of the aliens disguised as children. Ask, 'What does an alien look like?' Design new greetings to use when meeting an alien. Use signs and symbols and paint on a large piece of curtain lining. Attach to poles or hang from a wall.

- Ask the children to imagine they have time travelled and landed on a new planet. Ask them to write a description of what is seen, heard, smelt and tasted there. They should imagine that they've become space explorers and create a whole new world in their text. Use the website www.nasa.gov/audience/forkids for inspiration.

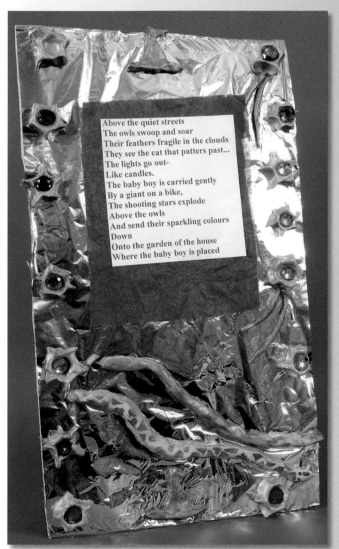

> Above the quiet streets
> The owls swoop and soar
> Their feathers fragile in the clouds
> They see the cat that patters past...
> The lights go out-
> Like candles.
> The baby boy is carried gently
> By a giant on a bike,
> The shooting stars explode
> Above the owls
> And send their sparkling colours
> Down
> Onto the garden of the house
> Where the baby boy is placed

- What would an alien bring to Earth and what might a human need to take for an interplanetary visit? Ask the children to draw these items onto suitcase-shaped paper.

- Choose four images that are very visual from the text of *Harry Potter and the Philosopher's Stone* by J.K. Rowling, for example, a downpour of shooting stars, excitable people in strange robes, a cat reading a map, and owls dropping letters. All of these images are linked with the ability of the wizards to travel through time without being visible to human beings or 'muggles'. The children could choose one of the images and draw what they think it could look like within the border of an A4 sheet of paper. Inside the border, ask them to write about the image in any poetic format, for example, 'They swooped from the clouds, owls of white, brown and grey, the evening rustled with busy feathers...' Type out on an A4 sheet of paper and mount on a large piece of cardboard covered with silver tinfoil. Mould the original images from their poems out of clay. Once dry, paint and stick down as a border on the cardboard base.

- Present the children with a letter from a small creature from another planet. The letter asks the children to describe a rainforest to the creature to help him with his homework. Extend this by developing an email address for the children to use to reply to the small creature.

- Make a magic stone. In *Harry Potter and the Philosopher's Stone,* readers learn that this stone is magical. The stone will transform any metal into pure gold. Read extracts from the book and then use salt dough to make a class 'philosopher's stone'. When it's dry, paint it in metallic colours. Stick sparkling stones and sequins onto the 'magic' stone afterwards. Use the stone in circle time during a speaking and listening exercise where the children sit in a circle and the stone is passed along and, in turn, the child who holds the stone says, 'I am holding the Philosopher's stone and this is my wish...'

Cross-curricular Links

Design and Technology

- Create a moving picture featuring a character from the children's time travelling writing (see Further Activities). Draw four pictures of the same character with different expressions. Glue them onto a horizontal strip of card. Slot through spaces in a frame and pull the strip quickly to make the character move. As an extension idea, think of four powerful newspaper headlines to go with each expression. Make a large newspaper cover (from cardboard) and, using the moving character, ask children to talk through the responses of the character.

Maths

- Download and photocopy a range of currency, such as euros, pounds sterling and dollars. Reinforce the children's understanding of large and small amounts within a currency. Design a starship menu with unusual names for space food. Price the different space foods. Ask the children 'Which is the most expensive/cheapest food or drink?', 'Which item can you buy for under 50p?' and 'What is there on the menu that is more than 50p, yet under £1.00?' Ask them to choose items from the menu and to work out how much they would cost altogether.

- Fill a selection of boxes and tubs with sand, play dough, newspaper and so on, so that they are different weights. Have children weigh them using scales. Ask them to imagine they are on Dr Xargle's planet and things are half the weight, quarter of the weight and so on. Using calculators, ask the children to work out the weight of the various objects on the alien planet.

Art

- Have copies of *The Monster Bed by* Jeanne Willis and Susan Varley available. Each child is to investigate the different illustrations in the book. As a discussion starter, ask the class if these illustrations have a purpose. Using A4 sheets of paper, get the children to think of one particular section of the book that made an impact on them, for example, the wood, or a picture of the monsters. Read and identify images in this section. Use these to recreate a new design for a monster. Illustrate the new monster using a variety of art materials.

Science

- Ask the children to create a magic formula discovered during their time-travelling experience. Place a mixture of cornflour and water into paper bowls. The children should mix these up. If the mixture is hit with a metal spoon, it will go hard. If it is picked up gently, it will run through your fingers. If it is picked up and squeezed, it will turn to powder. Each child has a bowl of the mixture. They will become wizards if the mixture responds in certain ways. Dress the children as wizards and have them use pretend wands. Make up magic phrases to say over the mixture and then get them to play with the magic mixture.

- Create Dr Xargle's space rocket. Use a litre bottle of cola, a packet of mints and a large area outside. Place the mints inside the coke, and stand back. The mints will increase the gas in the coke and the bottle will shoot up into the air.

History

- Fill a small suitcase with pictures, artefacts and documentation such as postcards and letters. Get examples of these that stretch across several generations or focus upon a particular period in history, such as the 1930s or the Victorians. Keep the lid closed and place the suitcase in the middle of an empty area of the classroom. Have the children sit in a circle. Show them the suitcase and ask them to suggest what might be in it. Give them clues such as 'history'. Choose a child to open the suitcase and take out one item. They should pass it around the circle. Ask the children what they now think is in the suitcase. Repeat the process several times until there are numerous items out of the suitcase. Piece together the history of the contents of the suitcase. Tell the children that as they are looking at and studying each item, they are in fact time travelling back to a time when these items belonged to someone and were in use.

Dance

- Make a spaceship. Ask the children to work together in small groups to form a spaceship. Discuss how they will take off and how they will show this. Children should demonstrate their ideas to futuristic music, such as Pink Floyd's *Dark Side of the Moon*. Extend with all children forming a fleet of spaceships. They need to move around without crashing!

Rainforests

Starting Points

- Using the text (preferably a big book copy) of *Where the Forest Meets the Sea* by Jeannie Baker, discuss with the children what they can see in each of the large illustrations. Give them five things to find, for example, five animals in the undergrowth, five different types of bark on the tree trunks and five different shades of brown. Explain that the illustrations set out to show how rich and varied a rainforest can be. Split the children into small groups and give each group a copy of the book. Using labelling, children should spot as many nouns, adjectives, adverbs and so on, in the illustrations as they can and write these down. For example, nouns – trunks, leaves; adjectives – twisting vines, bumpy, peeling bark. This activity provides a bank of vocabulary for further writing activities.

- Use the website www.rainforestweb.org/ as a starting point for discussion. Ask the children what they know and what they would like to find out about the rainforests. As a whole class, write down the knowledge they have and the questions they need answered. Write these questions down on small pieces of card and hand one to a pair. Their task is to find out ten facts about the key question that they will then share with the rest of the class.

Resources

- *Where the Forest Meets the Sea* by Jeannie Baker (Walker Books Ltd)
- CD: *Sounds of Earth: Rainforest* (Oreade Music)
- Atlases, maps and globes
- www.rainforestweb.org/
- www.fairtrade.org.uk
- www.exploratorium.edu/frogs/rainforest

Display

- Turn an area of the class into a rainforest. Suspend garden netting across the ceiling and hang tissue paper leaves from it. Thread vines made of rolled newspaper wrapped in brown tissue paper. Attach small insects and snakes to the vines and the netting.

- Get large branches and twigs and staple them to the wall. Make a tissue paper parrot and other rainforest animals and stick them onto the branches or the wall of the display area.

- Place a tape recorder or CD player in the area and play music, for example, *Sounds of Earth: Rainforest*.

Further Activities

- How can the children save the rainforests? Discuss the many animals that live in the canopies of the rainforests – katydids, beetles, parrots, toucans, cockatoos, anteaters, monkeys, sloths, macaws, butterflies, insects, boas. Ask them to imagine they are a rainforest animal that has been given the power of speech. What would they say to humans about the destruction of the rainforest? Collage a large picture of the animal with a speech bubble coming out of its mouth. Write suggestions for saving the rainforest inside the speech bubble.

- Write a fictional rainforest story based on non-fiction materials.

- Play Rainforest Word Scrabble. Children should be in small groups of four or five. Each group is given five rainforest-related words to jumble. Each group then takes turns and writes them on the board. The other groups try to guess what the words spell. Whichever group gets it first, gets a point. After the first group's words are correctly un-jumbled, the next group gets up to write their words and so on. The group with the most points wins.

- Write different types of letters (persuasive, business, informal) regarding the rainforests. For example, write a business letter to the president of a corporation responsible for destructive logging in the Amazon and persuade him or her to switch to sustainable forms of logging or alternative fibres altogether.

- Look at different brands of coffee especially the Fairtrade products. Have a selection of coffee available. Look at the marketing labels, the ingredients and the persuasive text on the jars. The children could compare the marketing strategies and select one they think is the most convincing. Research likes and dislikes of adults using an opinion poll. Research the history of Fairtrade at www.fairtrade.org.uk. Visit local stores to see who promotes Fairtrade products (Oxfam). Compose a letter to send to a supermarket chain persuading them to stock Fairtrade products.

Cross-curricular Links

Geography

- Where are the rainforests? Using atlases and websites, find the tropics, equator and rainforests. Get a blank map of the world. Colour the rainforests green. Search the atlas for desert areas and colour them yellow. Colour in black where the children live.

- What is the climate of a rainforest like? Investigate and compare using line graphs.

- Why are people cutting down the rainforests? Investigate and link up with schools in the Americas who are proactive in helping the rainforests.

- Investigate where the rainforests lie. What key features do they all have? Find three types of butterfly, monkey and small mammals that are found in one of these rainforests, such as Brazil.

- Investigating the layers. Show the class the book *Where the Forest Meets the Sea* by Jeannie Baker. Focus on the pictures that show all the layers of the forest, from the top layers of the canopy to the undergrowth. Focus the discussion on the colours, textures and shapes.

We tie-dyed using beetroot, tea and mint. We made feely bags with our material.

Art

- People living in the rainforest areas of the world use natural plants and materials to create medicines and natural fabric dyes. Take squares of cotton cloth. Place pebbles or small objects on the cloth, fold the cloth so the object is concealed and wrap an elastic band tightly to secure the object. This gives great tie-dye patterns once the fabric has been dyed and dried. Boil beetroot. Use the juice to dye white cloth. Do the same with cabbage/grass/turmeric/tea bags. Compare the strengths of the dyes. Use paints to duplicate the tones. Make feely bags with the fabric. Place textured objects inside them and link with literacy discussion tasks.

- Paint a backdrop of blue sky and green canopy. On a separate sheet of paper, paint a canopy and trunks. Cut out the shapes and stick them in 3-D relief over the backdrop. Draw and colour the animals, insects and birds that would be found in the rainforest. Glue them onto the parts of the forest where they would live.

RE

- The Yanomami Indians from the rainforest believe everything has a spirit and these spirits must be respected. Shamans are healers, they dance and sing to call good spirits to help one's illnesses. They use medicines made from the plants in the rainforest. Look at native artefacts from cultures living in rainforest conditions. Can the children use pottery, sketches or other mediums to explore these examples?

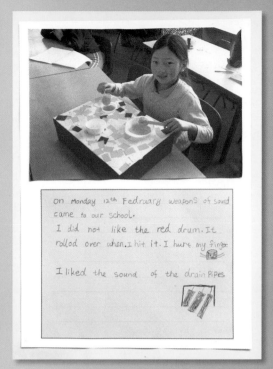

Science

- Create a rainforest ecosystem in the classroom. Decide what to plant in a terrarium/large fish tank. Place gravel in the base and cover with charcoal and compost. Plant sun plants, shade plants and vines. Spray the plants with distilled water and cover. Place the terrarium in a sunny place. Drops of water will start to form showing that the rainforest is functioning.

- Create a web of life. Use a ball of wool to illustrate a point. Gather students into a circle. Keeping hold of the beginning of the thread, have a child throw the ball of wool across the room to another child. That child then throws it to another and so on until a web has been formed. Ask the first student to pull on their piece of yarn. Do the rest of the class feel the pull? Explain how in the web of life, everything is interconnected. Extend by looking at food webs and chains in the rainforests.

Music

- Compose and perform some rainforest music using a variety of instruments. Plastic cups are ideal – cover them in tissue paper and place small seeds inside. Cover the opening with cling film, and shake. Use symbols to depict where and when a particular sound or instrument is needed. Get the children to devise and perform a dance to accompany their music. Tape record or video their musical and dance.

- Make a large banner using cloth. Place strips of masking tape down to form the letters 'Funky Junk' and the borders. Paint the fabric using fabric paints. When the paint is dry, remove the masking tape to reveal the white lettering and borders. Use this as a back cloth to display instruments made from recycled plastic bottles, cups for shakers, and a cereal box with cups placed in it to make a big shaker.

Electricity

Starting Points

- Investigate the invention of the light bulb. Research the life and work of the inventor Thomas Edison (1847–1931). More information about Edison can be found on the website www.invention.smithsonian.org/centerpieces/edison.

- Have a selection of light bulbs, including energy-saving light bulbs, for the children to look at. Ask the children to find out what types of bulbs are used in school and at home.

Resources

- *The Lighthouse Keeper's Lunch* by David Armitage and Ronda Armitage (Scholastic Hippo)
- *www.invention.smithsonian.org/centerpieces/edison*
- *www.andythelwell.com/blobz/guide.html*

Display

- Back a display board using red paper. Create a border using electrical cable tape. Add a large label saying 'Electricity' in the centre. Display a selection of photos showing how electricity is made with a short description for each. Display pictures of batteries and other electrical objects such as computers.

- Produce a series of cards with questions on them linked to the display, for example, 'What is a meter used for?' and 'What shape is a power station?' The children should use the display to answer the questions.

Further Activities

- Read a fiction story that includes the use of electricity, for example, *The Lighthouse Keeper's Lunch* by David Armitage and Ronda Armitage. Turn a corner of the classroom into a display for *The Lighthouse Keeper's Lunch*. Back a wall in blue paper in front of a unit or table top. Staple white waves onto the paper. Beneath these, sponge paint rolling waves. Ask the children to make pictures of boats and tuck them into the waves. Make seagulls by stuffing a white sock with newspaper and attaching two triangles of orange card for the beak. Sew on two black or brown beads for the eyes. Attach by using a strip of brown cardboard painted with white streaks or use a paintbrush and flick white paint onto the strip. Make a circular lighthouse out of card and paint in red and white stripes. Place a 2-D cut-out of the lighthouse keeper at the top. Add a table top with equipment for the children to build their working circuits. Make sure the focus is on electricity by having a series of circuits available. Ask the children to use the equipment to make the bulb light up, to make a buzzer sound and to make a motor work. Have cards on the surface with circuit pictures to aid investigation.

- Read again to the children the story of *The Lighthouse Keeper's Lunch*. Set the scene: the children have been marooned on an island with a lighthouse but there is no electricity and it is in the middle of winter! How do they solve the problem of heating and light? Can they use some of the ideas from the text to solve the problem?

- Use plastic bottles with caps (one per child), a fish tank or a large basin. Ask the children to write letters of distress from their island and place them in the bottles; set the bottles in the tank or basin. Children should then take bottles (not their own) out of the water and read aloud the tales. After reading each tale, they can 'rescue' the author by using maps and story details to find approximately where he or she is stranded.

- Using templates of a bolt of lightning and a thunder cloud, ask the children to write a sensory poem about storms. Watch a video or go on the Internet and watch live shots of storms. Record initial thoughts such as adverbs and adjectives on pieces of paper and transfer these words into a storm poem.

Cross-curricular Links

Science

- Experiment with making electrical circuits using bulbs, batteries and wires. A useful website is www.andythelwell.com/blobz/guide.html where children can investigate through interactive activities how to make circuits work, how to make a switch and so on.

- Make a magic magnet using a nail, plastic-coated wire with 1cm of wire exposed at each end and a 9V battery. Wrap the wire around the nail. Touch the ends to the battery for 10 seconds. Hold the nail against a paper clip. Ask the children to explain what happens.

- What uses electricity in the home? Draw a cross-section of a two-storey home with empty rooms. Ask the children to draw and label all electrical items found in those rooms.

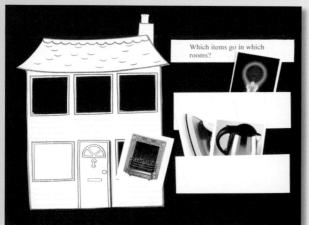

- Carry out a test of static electricity. The resources needed are a balloon and two cola cans (one empty and one full). Blow up a balloon and rub it on your head to build up a charge. Place an empty cola can horizontally on a smooth surface and slowly bring the charged balloon close to the can. Observe what happens and record using illustrations. Repeat the experiment using a full can of cola. Record what happened this time and why.

- Safety first! Contact a local electricity board and invite a speaker in to talk about the dangers of electricity and how to keep safe.

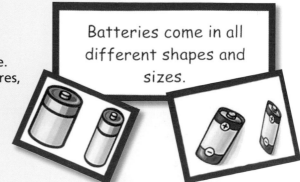

Batteries come in all different shapes and sizes.

- Have a selection of plugs disconnected from appliances and small screwdrivers. Take a plug apart. Discuss the wires and their purpose. Focus on the safety wire. Children are to draw the plug and the wires, labelling where they go and why.

⚠ **Note:** The children should be reminded not to do this to plugs that are connected to appliances, and also be reminded of the dangers of mains electricity.

Maths

- Create a magnetic maths game. Use the lid of a shoebox. Draw a road, race track, Grand-Prix circuit on the inside. Decorate with colours and small models of trees and so on. Stick small drawings of cars and horses onto paper clips. Using a magnet underneath the lid, move the cars and horses along the track. Invent a game based on rewards and consequences, for example, if you land on number 6 you have to recite the four times table; if you land on 9 you have to do a sum and so on.

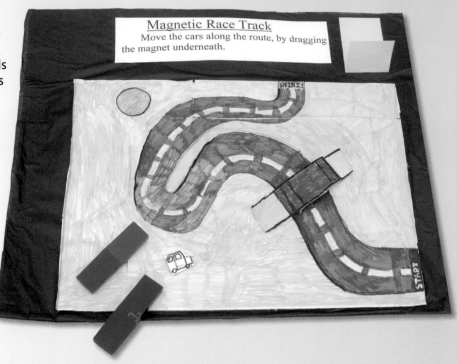

History

- Ask the children to look around the classroom or their home to find examples of toys which move without electricity. Can they work out what type of forces they use to move?

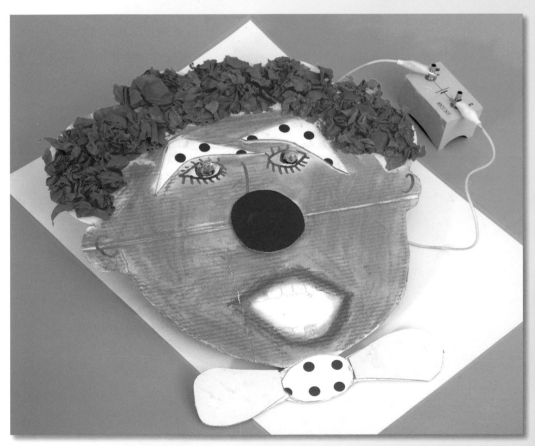

- Investigate toys through the ages. Focus on Victorian inventions that do not use electricity. Make a cardboard body with arms and legs attached with split pins to the body. Attach string to the arms and knees. Attach the string to a garden stake to make a puppet. Make a similar puppet of Punch and Judy. Research a script from Victorian Britain and enact the play.

Art and Design

- Draw a picture of a clown head and stick it onto card. Make a circuit with bulbs and batteries. Place the bulbs inside the card where the eyes are. Extend by using a motor that makes the clown's tie spin around.

Spiders

Starting Points

- Research spiders in popular movies, stories, songs, myths, poems and nursery rhymes. For example, Miss Muffet was a real girl. Her father, Thomas Muffet, made his daughter eat mashed spiders when she was sick. This remedy was used to cure colds 200 years ago.

- Read *Anansi the Spider* by Gerald McDermot and ask the children, 'Why does Anansi have so many adventures and what is the moral of the tale?' Explore morality in fables/myths and legends. Compare the story with the nursery rhymes of Western culture in which a cautionary message is hidden, warning children of poor behaviour and so on.

Display

- Make a large spider out of card. Colour it in with chalk. Stuff newspaper underneath the spider. Mount in the centre of the board on yellow paper. Cut out a series of spider webs for the border. Print questions linked to spiders and paste on backing paper. Use these as discussion starters.

- Make an in-tray from a piece of card. Place pieces of paper into this for the children to write on when answering the questions on the main display.

- Use the questions on the display to investigate non-fiction facts about spiders. The children could then explore these in detail using non-fiction books, for example, 'How do spiders spin their webs?', 'Where are the most poisonous spiders found?' and 'How do spiders lay their eggs?'

Resources

- *Anansi the Spider* by Gerald McDermot (Henry Holt & Co)
- *Spider-Man: The Amazing Story* by Catherine Saunders (DK Publishing)
- *Spiders* by Paul Hillyard (Harper Collins Publishers)
- *The Gruffalo* by Julia Donaldson (Macmillan Children's New Ed edition)
- www.marvel.com

Further Activities

- Design a PowerPoint presentation on a type of spider, for example, from Australia, South America or England. Link with non-fiction research in Literacy and food chains in Science. Include key details of habitat, breeding, food and so on.

- Read *Spider-Man: The Amazing Story* by Catherine Saunders. Discuss the character of Spiderman. Investigate the qualities of Peter Parker who turned into Spiderman. Make a 3-D comic strip depicting the moment Peter changes into Spiderman. Use speech bubbles to explain the change. Create a display to show the children's superhero. Back a display board with purple paper. Display descriptions of superheroes or favourite characters from TV and books together with key descriptive words of what superhero characteristics are, for example, strong, changes, good, powerful and so on.

- 'Hot seat' a child as the spider, and another as the fly. Think of as many valid points as to why the spider should not eat the fly and vice versa. Give a reward of a plastic spider to the child/ team with the best argument.

- Investigate cult comics such as Marvel. Log on to www.marvel.com and follow the link to digital comics. The comic pages will turn, allowing the children to read and study the text and illustrations online. Focus on the use of short sentences for descriptions by the 'narrator' and also the use of 'sound words'. Ask the children to create their own comic strip featuring a spider character.

- Research the history of superheroes such as Peter Parker, also known as Spiderman. Using the information you find out, write a CV description of the superhero.

Spider Man

Name: Peter Parker a.k.a: Spider Man

Date of birth: 9.05.1990 **Gender:** male

Identifying features: He has a red and blue suit. He has black eyes and black boots.

Special powers: He can spin webs with his hands. He is very strong.

History: He has saved a lot of people in the past and gets into lots of fights and he has saved the world from danger.

Address: 15 Rose ash lane

Description of neighbourhood: very colourful ,expensive cars.
Contacts: Mary Jane/ mamma.

Cross-curricular Links

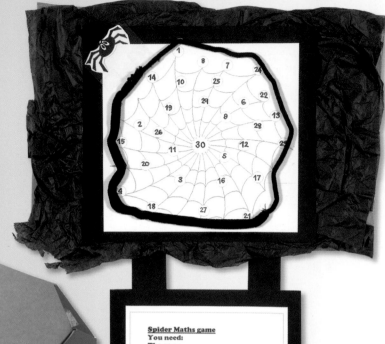

Maths

- Spider maths. Create a game for two players. Draw an A4-sized web. Put the numbers 1–29 on the web strings and the number 30 in the middle. Cut out and laminate two spiders. These take the place of the counters. Player one should throw two dice, add the numbers to reach a total and place the spider on the total number. Player two should then take their turn. The person to reach the centre of the web, the number 30, is the winner.

- Investigate eight-sided shapes. Take an octagon template and cut out several shapes. Stick them together until the 3-D shape resembles a football. Investigate the success of such a shape, for example, how far each ball can roll, be kicked and travel down slopes. Record findings.

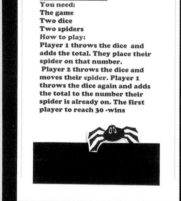

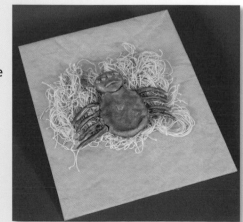

Science

- Investigate the food chain of a spider. Use words such as predator, prey, consumer and producer. Extend by reading *The Gruffalo* by Julia Donaldson and explore food chains such as mouse eaten by fox or owl.

- Investigate arachnids with attitude! Discuss which spiders are the most venomous. (Black widow spider and Wandering spider.) Do they have any useful habits? (They keep down the population of the fly and so on.)

- Using disposable cameras, set the children a challenge: find and photograph the largest spider web without disturbing the spider. It helps to lightly spray the web beforehand with water. Print the photos and ask the children to describe in detail the shapes of the web and what was trapped in the web. Extend the activity by asking the children to write in the first person narrative of the spider, describing how great giants (children) came so close to his habitat.

Design and Technology

- Investigate web design. Using plastic hoops, set the children a task to design the strongest web they can using wool, string and fishing wire. The web has to hold a weight successfully – these could be tinned food, soft toys and so on. To make it a fair test, all the hoops have to use the same object. The children should share their design ideas with the rest of the class.

- Ask the children to design their own spider and consider the habitat, climate and what types of enemies the spider might have. How will it survive in its habitat? Will it be diurnal or nocturnal? Will it live above or underground? Design a 2-D model on graph paper and then draw a scale model of the spider. Extend the activity by making a 3-D model using clay and naming the spiders.

Art and Design

- Make a web. Use cardboard as a base. Draw a large circle on the card. Pierce the centre with a knitting needle. Pierce holes at equal intervals around the circle. Using thread, wool or fishing wire, pass a needle from the centre in and out of the circumference to make a 'wheel design'. Use tinsel or sparkly thread to weave in and out of the 'spokes'. Complete the web by adding sequins as raindrops on the 'spokes'. Make a pom-pom spider to sit in the centre. Use the webs as a stimulus for poetry. For example, 'My spider sits in the web like…, My spider moves on the web like…, My spider jumps on the web like…, My spider sleeps on the web like…, My spider waits on the web like…'

- Give each pair of children a shoebox and tell them to create a 'superhero' setting within the box. Use card to create 3-D buildings. Suspend card figures of superheroes from fishing wire strung across the top of the shoebox. Use the setting to inspire free writing about a superhero.

Dance and Drama

- How do spiders move? Build a web out of skipping ropes. Ask the children to explore travelling across the 'web'. What parts of their bodies do they use most? Give each child a sheet of newspaper to stand on. When music plays, they should move in a spider-like way until it stops and then find another sheet to stand on. Remove a sheet each time the music ends. They should change how they move each time – crawling, skittering, jumping and sidling sideways. If a child has no sheet to stand on when the music stops, they must sit out. The winner is the child left on the last sheet of newspaper.

PSCHE

- Put the children into pairs. One child is the spider and the other the fly. Think of an argument to use as the fly to dissuade the spider from eating it. For example, 'I'm too small; a bluebottle would be better' or 'Isn't it time you turned vegetarian?'

- Hold a Spider Court. Select a jury of flies and spiders. The accused is the spider and the defendant is the fly. Discuss the matter of the spider eating the fly's brother. How well can the spider and the fly argue their points of view? How will the jury decide? Record (visual or audio) the courtroom session of the trial of the spider and the fly.

Teeth

Starting Points

- Read the text of *I Know Why I Brush My Teeth (Sam's Science)* to the class. Discuss the children's views on brushing their teeth. Ask, 'Why do we do it?', 'Who has been to a dentist?' and 'Why do we need teeth?' Record the children's ideas onto a flip chart.

- Have a selection of toothbrushes, toothpastes and dental floss available. Ask the children what they like about their brushes, what their favourite toothpaste is and why we floss. Put the children into pairs. Give each pair a mirror and a whiteboard and pens. They will look into their mouths and make a note of everything they see. The pair that spots the most things can get a 'Smile' certificate.

Display

- Create a mouth using red tissue paper. Back tissue paper with newspaper to create a 3-D effect. Stick a large piece of tongue-shaped paper from the opening of the mouth. Stick key words on it: incisor, molar, tear, chew, mouth, saliva and so on.

- Cut out small mouths from red paper and use them as a border around the display board.

- Print off and mount tooth facts and hang them from the board on card so they stand out. Add information about gums and teeth and print out pictures of healthy gums and teeth. Add facts about teeth hygiene – brushing regularly, flossing and visiting the dentist. Add information about the sugar content of certain foods such as sugary drinks and canned foods. Type these out and display under the heading of 'Did You Know?'

Resources

- *I Know Why I Brush My Teeth (Sam's Science)* by Kate Rowan (Walker Books Ltd)
- *The Three Little Wolves and the Big Bad Pig* by Eugenios Trivizas (Prentice Hall & IBD)
- *Little Red Riding Hood* (Ladybird Books Ltd)
- *Willy the Wimp* by Anthony Browne (Walker Books Ltd)
- *Willy the Champ* by Anthony Browne (Walker Books Ltd)

Further Activities

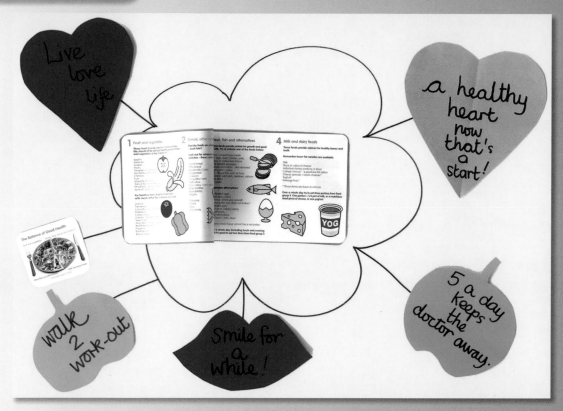

- Healthy bodies and lifestyles. Investigate how many teeth we have and what types they are. What do we use our teeth for? How do we look after them? Why do we need them? How are they linked to keeping our bodies healthy? What are milk teeth? Record the children's ideas. Look at a brochure highlighting the 5 A DAY principle. In groups, they decide what a healthy diet will do for their health and well-being. List these on templates of a heart, an apple and smiling lips, for example, 'Live, love, life' on a template of a heart.

- Read the text of *The Three Little Wolves and the Big Bad Pig* by Eugenios Trivizas, discuss how the author has altered the tale by making the wolves the goodies. Explore the illustrations and compare the dark humour of the dynamite using pig to the non-humorous traditional character of the wolf in *Little Red Riding Hood*.

- Read Willy the Wimp and Willy the Champ by Anthony Browne. Discuss 'Why does toothpaste help our dental hygiene?', 'What food do we chew and digest?' and 'How does this make us healthy?'

- Create a character based on the tooth fairy. Create a setting such as under the pillow. Give the character a challenge such as: children are eating much healthier foods and are therefore losing less teeth. Ask, 'What problems does this pose to the tooth fairy and how would she/he resolve the situation?'

- Give each child a mirror and ask them to look at their own teeth. Discuss how teeth can be healthy – brushing, flossing, healthy food intake and so on.

- Produce an advertisement for a new type of crisp which is salt and fat free, has no additives, has interesting tastes and colours, and that is good for your teeth. The children should use persuasive wording on the advert, for example, 'What could a potato do for you?' Extend by having children produce an advertising jingle and linking it with their product. They could produce a PowerPoint presentation using the ideas generated in Literacy for an advertisement for a new crisp including headline, subtext, picture of product and healthy lifestyle options.

Cross-curricular Links

Maths

- Have a marvellous maths tasting session. Give each group (four per group) a selection of crisps. Each child rates the taste of the crisps on a scale of 1–5, with 5 being an enjoyable taste and 1 being the least enjoyable. Then, using a graph, record the children's findings, firstly per group and then the whole class. Use the results from the survey to produce a class bar graph or extend to the more able by completing a scatter graph.

Art and Design

- Talk about foods that are good for teeth and health in general. Using the children's ideas, draw large vegetables onto a large sheet of canvas which has been divided into co-ordinate sections. Put masking tape around the drawings and then use fabric paints to colour in the vegetables. Use 'earth colours' for the background. Display as a large banner in a hall.

- Using toothpaste, create pictures on card of swirls, circles and ovals. Investigate what types of realistic pictures children can invent using only toothpaste. How could they improve their ideas? What other medium could they use?

Science

- What can you taste? Have a selection of foods that are salty, bitter and sweet. Children sample foods and try to work out which parts of their tongue they can taste these foods on. Label a picture of the tongue to show these areas.

 Note: Some children may be allergic to one or more of the foods, so check with guardians for any allergies.

- Using the Internet, investigate who invented toothpaste. Was it always in a tube? What did people use before the invention of the tube?

- Try a tooth experiment. Use mouthwash, three eggs, vinegar and three bowls. Pour mouthwash into one of the bowls with an egg. Leave for ten minutes. Remove the egg. Pour four inches of vinegar into each of the remaining two bowls. Put the mouthwash and egg into one bowl of vinegar and the other egg in another bowl of vinegar. One egg will start to bubble as the vinegar (an acid) starts to attack the minerals in the egg shell. Which egg will start to bubble? Children should explain this

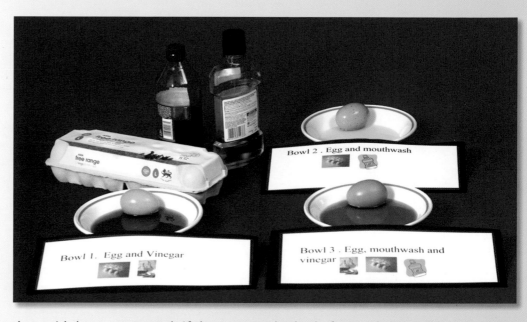

result. This simulates the effect that acids have upon teeth if they are not looked after and cleaned regularly.

- Discuss what acid does to teeth. Use two clean chicken bones (as teeth), a plastic bowl and white vinegar. Pour several inches of vinegar into the bowl. Soak the clean chicken bones in the vinegar overnight. What has happened overnight? Are they softer or harder?

Design and Technology

- Design a toothbrush that will reach all the parts of the mouth and the tongue.

- Invent toothpaste that is easy to squeeze.

- Make a 3-D rectangular net of a tooth box or package that is easy to put under the pillow for the tooth fairy to find. Stick the net together with double-sided adhesive and cover in tissue paper. Stick beads and sequins to the outside of the box. It can now be used to store a child's baby teeth in.

- Make an edible mouth. Slice an apple into six parts. Spread peanut butter on two slices. Stick small marshmallows onto them. Stick the slices together to make a mouth and eat!

- Design and make a 3-D mouth with teeth. Velcro labels on the different teeth and tongue. Make pictures of the different types of food that are chewed by the teeth – molars for grinding, canines for ripping and so on. Make this an interactive display with question cards.

Weather

Resources

- *Learning about Weather (Scienceworks for Kids Series)* by Jo Ellen Moore (Evan-Moor Educational Publishers)
- *Little Cloud* by Eric Carle (Putnam Publishing Group)
- DVD: *The Wizard of Oz* (Warner Home Video)
- DVD: *The Polar Express* (Warner Home Video)
- www.fema.gov
- www.the-north-pole.com

Starting Points

- Using the Internet, books and magazines, ask the children to find out about floods. Focus on the plight of individual people and the efforts of volunteers during floods.

- Become weather watchers. The children will need an observation chart and a pencil. At the start of each day (for a week), stand the class outside for approximately five to ten minutes making group observations of the weather. Ask questions such as 'What is the reason behind the air feeling hot or cold?' and 'Why are clouds different shapes?' Record observations and return to the classroom. On day two, give each child a square of card with a square cut out in the middle (a 'weather watcher'). They look through the small square in the centre of the 'watcher' and record what they see in picture form. Label or annotate afterwards.

The Desert

The desert is a huge piece of land covered in sand. It is very dry and often there is no water for miles.
Camels are used by people to carry items across the desert. They store water in their humps and can survive for weeks without drinking water.

Display

- Back a board in blue. Using papier mâché, make a 3-D half circle to represent the world. With tissue paper, make flat shapes to show the continents. Place in the centre of the board. Attach photographs of people from other countries and link with string to parts of the world such as West Africa and North Africa. Add text under the photos with lift-up flaps.

- Make a daily weather chart. Place weather symbols into a pocket stapled to the wall. Attach Velcro to the symbols.

Further Activities

- Research, using TV reports and the Internet, the aftermath of Hurricane Katrina that devastated New Orleans in 2005. Try the website www.fema.gov.

- Watch an extract from *The Wizard of Oz,* where the hurricane strikes the house that Dorothy is in and transports her to the land of Oz. Ask the children to write down their responses to the images. They should think about how Dorothy felt. Watch the film up to where it changes from black and white to colour. They should come up with a reason as to why this was done. (The black and white part of the film represents the real time that Dorothy is living in, and the coloured part of the film shows Dorothy in the fantasy world of Oz after the tornado picks up her house.)

- *The Polar Express* deals with winter and snow and a magical journey to the North Pole. Watch the film and get children to explore the childhood wonder of Christmas and imagination. What makes Christmas so important? Why is the North Pole important to the idea of Christmas? Explore the idea of the North Pole being the home of Father Christmas. Visit the website www.the-north-pole.com. Use the email site to write letters to Santa. Examine the main characters in the film – the boy, the little girl and the train conductor. What is the target audience of the film? Describe the weather on the journey to the North Pole and the types of animals that are seen in the film – wolves, eagles and so on.

- Discuss the seasons with the children. In pairs, ask the children to paint pictures of the seasons, concentrating on colours, what is growing in that season and what the weather traditionally is, for example, winter snow, autumn golden leaves. Display the pictures.

- The children could draw or paint pictures showing weather types – sunny, snowing, drizzle, thunderstorns and so on. Display in an oval shape with two movable pointed clock hands in the centre. Children can move the hands to show what the weather is like on each day.

Science

- Make wind chimes using a variety of small metal objects like nuts, bolts, washers, screws, nails, jar lids, fishing line of various lengths 25–28cm, scissors and a tree branch on a windy day. Tie one end of a piece of fishing line to each metal object. Tie the other end of each of the fishing lines to the tree branch so the objects hang freely. Tie two additional pieces of fishing line of the same length to each end of the tree branch to use to hang your wind chime from your favourite tree.

- Demonstrate evaporation of water from a puddle. On a sunny day, pour a cup of water on the playground. Ask the children to draw a circle around the perimeter with chalk. Leave for 30 minutes before checking on the puddle. Ask the children where the water went and why. Write a story about the disappearing water: it has gone on a journey and will return in a little while somewhere else in the world. Read *Little Cloud* by Eric Carle for inspiration.

- Investigating water erosion, create a 'canyon' on a deep tray by filling it with soil. Set the tray at a low angle. Slowly pour water on the soil. Place the cup (filled with water) at the high end. The water will create a small canyon in the pan.

Art and Design

- Take a piece of white paper and wet it with water. Drip paint onto it and spread the colour across the bottom of the page. Let it dry and then place blobs of black ink on the bottom. Take a straw and blow through it onto the black ink so it makes streaks like branches on the paper. Continue until you have several trees. Vary the direction to show trees blowing in the wind.

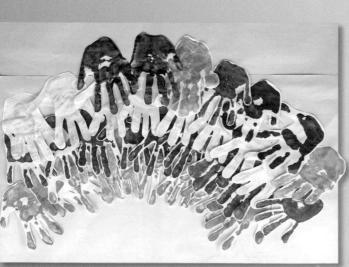

- Photocopy a sheet showing satellite pictures of hurricanes. Use clear plastic sheeting, glass paint, wool, sticky paper and tissue paper. Ask the children to show the swirling circular movements of the hurricane by using any of the materials, stuck down onto the plastic sheets. Display against a window.

- Discuss the colours of the rainbow and mix up the shades with the class. Each child should choose a colour and paint their hand with that colour. Make hand prints on paper. Cut out the hand prints and place in an arch shape to make a class rainbow. Extend by asking children to write about what they can do with their hands and display their writing underneath the 'hand' rainbow.

Design and Technology

- Make a collection of fruit for each colour of the rainbow in a large bowl. Ask the children to call out the colours of the rainbow, then take the colour fruit out of the bowl. Pass the foods around, explaining that the foods are very nutritious which help children grow and stay healthy. Using one rainbow colour at a time, ask the children to name nutritious foods that are that colour. The children could search through magazines for foods that match the colours in the bowl.

- Ask the children to write weather poems on weather templates. Hang these from a mobile. Join two coat hangers together and wrap with white tissue paper. Suspend weather symbols (rainbow, lightning, raindrops, sun) from the mobile too.

Maths

- Record the temperature. Have thermometers available in the class. Place both outside and inside the classroom. Read the temperature on the thermometer at specific times in the day and record on a chart next to the thermometers. Discuss 'Is it hotter outside?' and 'Why is it hotter near the radiator than next to the windows and so on?' Extend the activity by asking each child to draw a thermometer.

- Look at negative numbers, count up and down from the positives to the negatives, for example, –5°C added to 7°C equals 2°C.

- Each child should be provided with a compass and a piece of paper, card and a ruler. The children should practise using compasses and draw circles. Stick the end of the compass into the paper and secure it in a piece of card underneath the paper (this stops it moving about). Show them a picture of the eye of a hurricane and ask them to reproduce the image using a compass. Extend by saying the distance across the eye is 5cm, 7cm and 10cm. Children extend the compass arms to the distance and draw the circles.

Body Bits

Starting Points

- Read a non-fiction text on the human body such as *Human Body* (*DK Eyewitness Guides*) by Steve Parker. If possible, look at pages showing internal organs, joints, blood vessels and how the eye works.

- Ask the children to write a set of funny instructions with the title 'How to put together my body'. They should use bullet points and add simple illustrations. For example, 'My head goes on my elbow which is attached to my foot. My eyes are on the side of my head, and my nose is on top of my knee.'

Display

Resources

- *Human Body (DK Eyewitness Guides)* by Steve Parker (Dorling Kindersley Publishers Ltd)
- *Billy McBone* from *Heard it in the Playground* by Allan Ahlberg (Puffin Books)
- *Animal Dreaming: An Aboriginal Dreamtime Story* by Paul Morin (Silver Whistle)
- *Funnybones* by Allan Ahlberg (Puffin Books: New Ed edition)
- www.haringkids.com
- www.globalclassroom.org
- www.dreamtime.auz.net

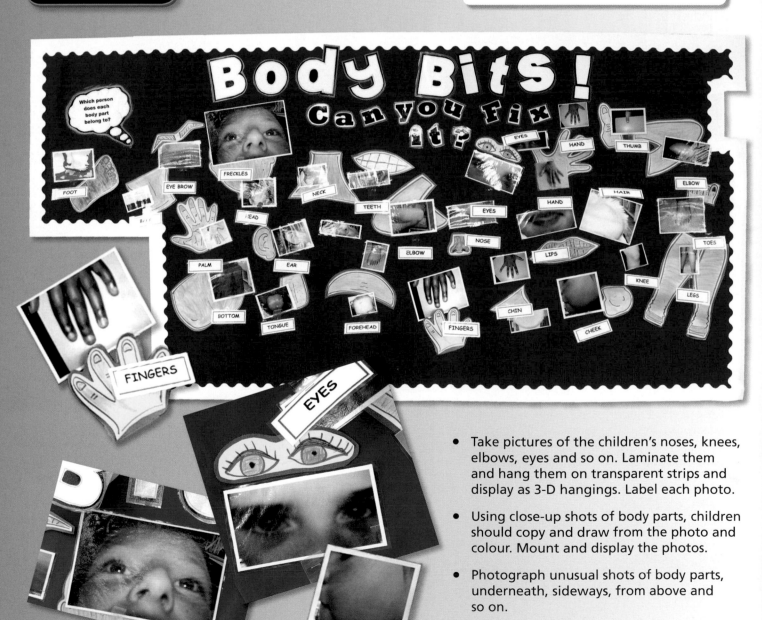

- Take pictures of the children's noses, knees, elbows, eyes and so on. Laminate them and hang them on transparent strips and display as 3-D hangings. Label each photo.

- Using close-up shots of body parts, children should copy and draw from the photo and colour. Mount and display the photos.

- Photograph unusual shots of body parts, underneath, sideways, from above and so on.

Further Activities

- Discuss the journey that food takes from the moment the children eat it. Put this into a fairy tale narrative form, for example, 'Once upon a time, a plate of food waited happily on the table. It was looking forward to going on a wonderful journey of discovery. It would be where it had never been before and would have wonderful adventures along the way…'

- Cut out a large mouth from red paper. Cut out a tongue and stick one end to the middle of the mouth. Paste the children's work onto the tongue.

- Read the poem *Billy McBone*, from *Heard it in the Playground* by Allan Ahlberg, to the class. Discuss the child in the poem – who no one could teach, whom the teachers thought was stupid, but who actually had wonderful thoughts that 'wandered free'. Use this as the basis for the children's own poems entitled 'Inside the head of a boy is…' and 'Inside the head of a girl is…' Extend beyond the usual gender stereotypical statements. Display the poems on silhouettes of the children's heads.

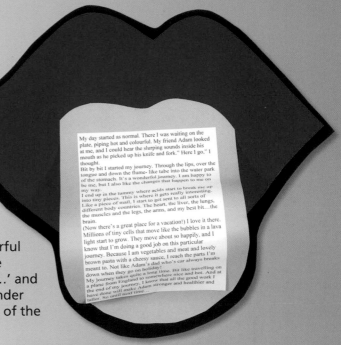

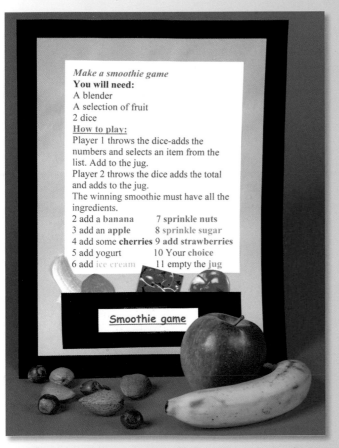

Cross-curricular Links

Maths

- This activity encourages the children to examine their bodies through measurement. Use tape measures or string to measure different parts of the body. Ask the children to record these measurements in centimetres. Make a newspaper model of a person using these measurements. Using newspaper and sellotape, roll the newspaper sheets into tubes and attach them with sellotape. Ideally, the children should make the spine first.

- Compare the heights of the children in the class. Encourage questions such as, 'If two children are the same height, do they have the same size heads, feet and so on?' Investigate similarities of length of arms and feet. These can then be used to produce graphs, bar charts and Venn diagrams, for example, four children with size three feet; ten children with the same length arms. There are many programmes in school and online that allow children to produce computer-generated graphs. Try www.globalclassroom.org for some ideas.

- After discussion about what makes our bodies stay healthy, create a Smoothie Game. Have copies of a sheet with a recipe for a smoothie on it, and cards printed with pictures of a sundae glass, two scoops of frozen yoghurt, slices of fruit (banana, strawberry, apple). Ask the children to work in pairs. Each child has a dice and for each number rolled they add pieces to their smoothie. The first person to collect the cards to make a complete smoothie (as shown on the recipe) is the winner. Paste the typed instructions onto firm card and make a holder strip at the base to store all the smoothie pieces in.

PSHCE

- Discuss what our bodies can do, for example, tap feet, clap hands, use our mouths and so on. Can we make drums of our bodies? Can we make our ears move? Ask each child the special things they can do with their bodies.

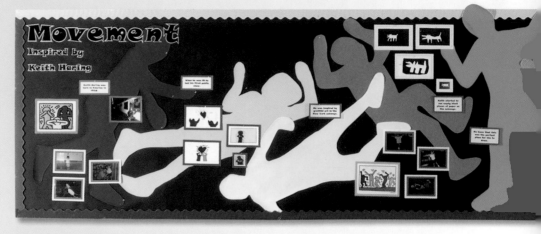

- Photocopy an A3-sized picture of a body. Draw jigsaw shapes on the picture. Cut out the pieces and put them in an envelope. In small groups, ask the children to take out a piece. They should find the matching pieces by asking questions such as, 'I have the head, what is the piece I need to make a body?' The child with the neck responds with 'I have the neck' and gives the piece to the child. The pieces could be stuck to a board. The skills involved in this activity include waiting their turn, listening and remembering the order of the body parts.

- Use the jigsaw pieces from the above activity in a whole-class reward system, with children being awarded a piece of jigsaw for good behaviour and so on. When the class has a whole body, they earn a whole-class reward, such as a bowl of fruit for the class.

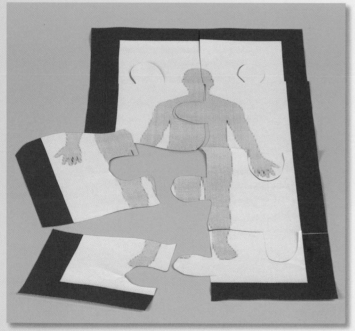

PE

- Discuss the function of our organs and why they are on the inside of our bodies. Ask questions such as, 'What are the jobs of the parts of our body?' and 'What jobs is your body really good at?' (for example, running, thinking, eating, writing, hugging). In groups, ask the children to make a shape like a heart using their bodies. They should then think of three words to describe what the heart does.

- Sit the children in a circle and ask them to close their eyes and listen to some music. They should think about what movements they can make with their bodies to the music. Join the movement together in pairs and extend the movements to create a sequence.

Science

- Using non-fiction texts and pictures projected onto the whiteboard, brainstorm with the children all the parts of the body – legs, arms, nose and so on. Write down each of the words on stick-it notes. Produce a life-size image of a child. Children should stick the labels onto the correct parts of the figure. Build up a word bank to include internal organs such as heart and stomach. What job does the stomach do?

- Your nose knows (investigate the relationship between taste and smell). Ask the children to close their eyes and pinch their nose. Tell them to place a sweet in their mouths while pinching their nose. Taste the sweet and ask what they feel, taste and smell. After 60 seconds, they should stop holding their nose and record any differences in taste, smell and feel.

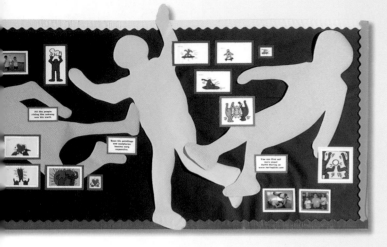

Art and Design

- Take a photograph of each child. (Obtain permission from the child's parent/guardian.) Photocopy these in black and white. Using craypas, ask the children to shade in shadow lines to enhance their features or change themselves completely.

- Look at body art, for example in *Animal Dreaming: An Aboriginal Dreamtime Story* by Paul Morin.

- Discuss the theme of the Creation story. Use the website www.dreamtime.auz.net/ to investigate other Dreamtime Creation stories and compare in written form to the story of how God made the world in seven days. Using flour, add a small amount of water. Place into a paint palette and add colours. This will be the basis of 3-D dreamtime art. On a piece of black sugar paper, draw with a pencil a series of interconnecting lines to make the outline of a body. Dip the end of a paintbrush into a paint colour and put a dot of paint/flour onto the pencil lines. Continue along the line. Allow to dry. Spray with hairspray to secure the paint.

- Cut out large child-sized coloured silhouettes of figures in different moving positions – running, skipping, diving for a ball. Use these as a central focus on a large display board in the hall. The children could draw simple outline pictures of sports, animals moving, shapes of hearts and kisses, and transfer designs to templates of card and display amongst the figures. Take photographs of children in PE and enlarge to add to the display.

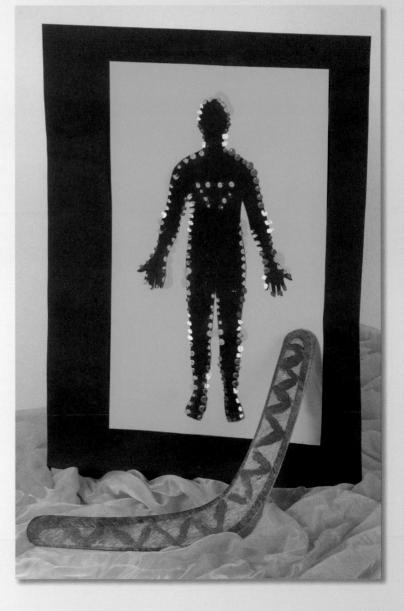

- Look at the work of Keith Haring (1958–99) using the website www.haringkids.com.image. Haring was a Pop Art artist, whose chalk work could be found all over the walls and billboards of the New York subway. His work became famous as a result, and until his death, much of his work dealt with love, happiness and communication between people. Discuss with the children his use of simple bold cartoon-like figures.

- Using an ICT programme such as Paint, get the children to create simple outlines of figures showing affection such as two silhouettes holding a heart. Infill with colour, print and mount. Place the smaller computer-generated images of love, friendship and animals amongst the larger figures on the display.

Design and Technology

- Make a skeleton puppet. Using the text of *Funnybones* by Allan Ahlberg, read through to the part where all the bones fall apart. Take a skeleton template. Children cut out the shapes and put them together in the right positions. Use split pins for the joints. Take some string and attach it to a joint and investigate how to make it skip or dance.

Ancient Egypt

Starting Points

- Use the website www.historyforkids.org/ as a starting point for information and background about Ancient Egypt.

- Ask the children to choose one area they wish to investigate, such as Egyptian people. Give each child a pre-prepared booklet (sugar paper is good for this). On the inside cover, make an envelope for any work they print off so they can refer back to it. They can record information in any way, such as cartoons, drawings, copying and pasting text from the screen. This should be used as their book for the project.

Resources

- *How to Prepare a Mummy* by Jillian Powell (Longman)
- www.historyforkids.org/
- www.guardians.net/egypt/kids/

Display

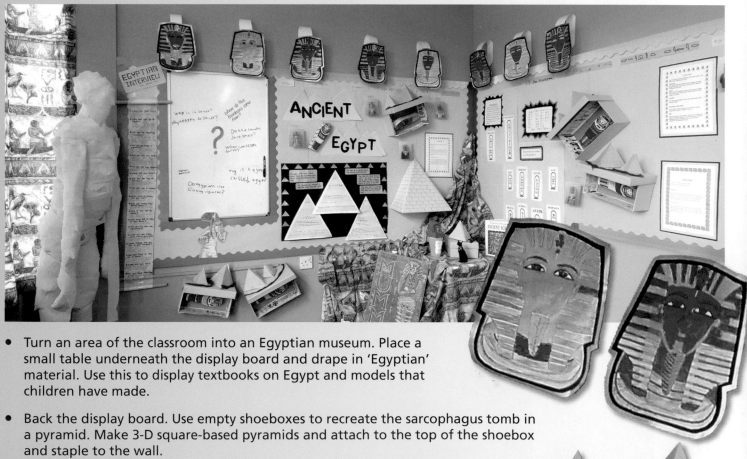

- Turn an area of the classroom into an Egyptian museum. Place a small table underneath the display board and drape in 'Egyptian' material. Use this to display textbooks on Egypt and models that children have made.

- Back the display board. Use empty shoeboxes to recreate the sarcophagus tomb in a pyramid. Make 3-D square-based pyramids and attach to the top of the shoebox and staple to the wall.

- Create headdresses of Pharaohs and display above the board.

- Ask the children to write their names in hieroglyphs and display on cream paper with an explanation of the work.

- Make several large square-based pyramids and attach to the display.

- Wrap a full-size skeleton in white toilet paper to act as a mummy to stand next to the display.

Further Activities

- Ask the children to use the Internet to find out about the life of a particular pharaoh. Pick out key features of their life and list on a flip chart. Ask the children to write a biography of the Pharaoh. Describe the reasons the Pharaoh was so important, such as wars that were won, cities that had been built, temples dedicated to a certain god.

- Using the website www.guardians.net/egypt/kids/ which has excellent links to websites on Egypt, both past and present, ask the children to choose an area to explore such as the link to the cyber journey of Egypt.

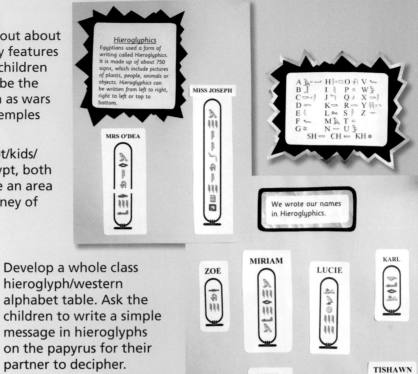

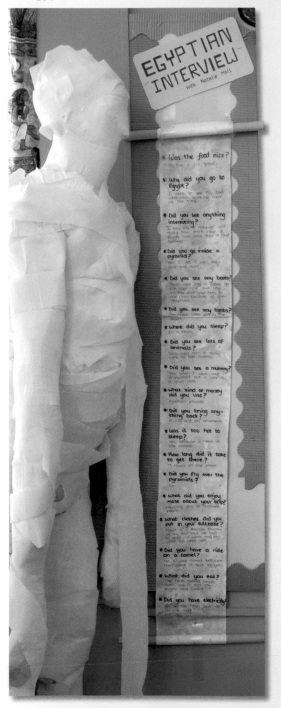

- Develop a whole class hieroglyph/western alphabet table. Ask the children to write a simple message in hieroglyphs on the papyrus for their partner to decipher. Discuss how archaeologists unlocked the mystery of this ancient written language.

- Attach several sheets of A4 paper together to make a long scroll. Using a damp teabag, stain the paper to age it. Roll each end around a piece of dowling. On whiteboards, children should write down any questions they might like to ask on the theme of Ancient Egypt. Type these out and use these as guides for children to research the answers. Write the answers underneath the questions and attach to the scroll.

- Write a simple message to the children in hieroglyphs. Have alphabet letters next to hieroglyphic symbols. Ask them to decipher this. This will allow discussion to develop about how ancient written signs and symbols were deciphered by archaeologists. Create messages using the alphabet/symbol code. The children could swap their messages with a partner. They could use the same alphabet to write their names in hieroglyphics.

- Choose texts about the Egyptian rites for burial, such as *How to Prepare a Mummy* by Jillian Powell. Use the children's recorded notes from the 'mummification' session in RE. Use this as a question and answer session. One child is the reporter on the Pyramid Post newspaper, who will interview one of the priests that conducted the ceremony. The report needs a brief headline, an illustration of the ceremony and an introductory paragraph.

- Visit the pyramids! Produce an Egyptian tour pamphlet (make available several holiday brochures with clear pictures – local travel agents will supply these). Include airfares, cruises, hotel accommodation, camel rides across the desert and so on.

Cross-curricular Links

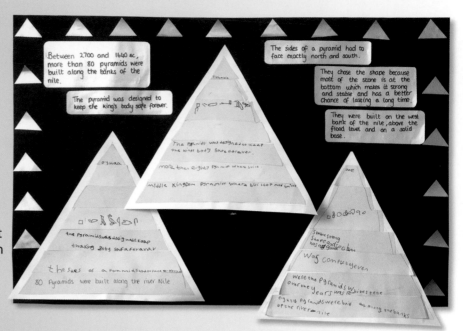

Maths

- Display a picture of a pyramid. Discuss 'How many sides, faces, edges in a triangle?' and ' How many triangles in a pyramid?' Use protractors to measure acute angles on a straight line. Transfer to producing triangles and build a pyramid. Draw lines to show bricks. Using the papyrus made in art, write down a description of how to build a pyramid out of triangles. Use mathematical words such as edge, face, angle and apex.

- Create a calendar. Ancient Egyptians created the calendar with 365 days. Investigate the science behind this and use to reinforce months, days, weeks, hours and so on. Extend by setting maths questions such as, 'If I set out from the pyramid of Cheops at 12.30, and it took me two hours to get to the hotel, what time would I arrive?'

Science

- Mummify an apple. Cut apples into slices. Coat each one in a different solution, for example, equal amounts of water and table salt, equal amounts of water and Epsom salts and equal amounts of water and baking soda. Place the apples in separate small bowls. The apples will start to mummify in a few days. Check each day to see which apple is mummifying quicker.

History

- Read the book *How to Prepare a Mummy* by Jillian Powell and discuss the images. Discuss why bodies were preserved. Look at evidence found in tombs, for example, Tutankhamen, on the Internet that shows that Egyptians believed they would lead a new life in the underworld.

- Take a shoebox and lid, wrap them in brown/cream paper. On the lid, place a large pyramid made in a maths lesson. Use a toothpaste box with the ends cut off so it curves inwards. Wrap it in white paper to make a sarcophagus and draw a detailed image of the Pharaoh on the top. Place in the shoebox tomb.

- Use the text from *How to Prepare a Mummy*. Choose one child to be a dead pharaoh. Lay the child on a table. The rest of the class role-play being priests who are present at the mummification. Pretend to light small tea lights and surround the body. Role-play the process of removing the organs and placing them into canopic jars. Afterwards, wrap the child in toilet paper. The class record the process on whiteboards in the form of bullet point notes.

Art and Design

- Make some papyrus. Take strips of 1cm wide by 30cm long paper and weave them together. Then soak in water and put heavy weights on it to flatten it. Or do as the Egyptians did and pound with stones to flatten it.

- Make clay tablets. Mix Plaster of Paris with water and brown paint. Pour the plaster mix into plastic takeaway containers. Leave until still soft to the touch. Using the end of a paintbrush or pencil tip, ask the children to engrave hieroglyphic characters into the mixture. When dry, use metallic and black paints to colour inside the engravings.

A human head for the liver
A falcon for the intestines
A baboon to look after the lungs
A jackal to look after the stomach

- Make canopic jars. Papier mâché around plastic cups. Place a piece of cardboard on the lip of the cup and papier mâché to hold. Using large clumps of papier mâché, mould the head of any of the Egyptian animal gods. Paint when dry.

- Make a wearable Pharaoh's headdress using a large piece of card cut out to make a headdress. Decorate in royal colours. Alternatively, make 3-D Egyptian Pharaoh masks using card. Cut out eyes and glue blue or black strips of paper down around the eyes to resemble kohl. Attach a triangular nose to the mask. Attach a headdress to the edge of the mask where the hairline is. Decorate the face using foil paper.

- Create some mummies. You will need newspaper, masking tape, cardboard and metallic paint. Roll newspapers into balls to create the outline of the 'mummy' and wrap with masking tape. Make a separate ball for the head and wrap with masking tape. Use strips of newspaper to create the nose and the eye sockets and wrap with tape. To make the sarcophagi, extend the mummy design by cutting a semicircle of cardboard and attach to the head of the mummy with tape. This will create the headdress. Build up the nose and, using several thick strips of newspaper, make the arms folded across the body. Using PVA glue and yellow tissue paper, cover the sarcophagus until no masking tape is visible. Allow to dry and paint or spray with metallic gold paint. Once dry, add eyeliner detail, diamond shapes for jewel decoration on main body and strips of blue shiny paper on the headdress. Display against a wall for support.

Design and Technology

- Make a mancala board from an empty egg carton. You need 48 playing pieces – small stones, seeds, marbles, shells or even small pieces of wood. Set up the board by placing four playing pieces in each hole. Each player has a 'store' on their end of the mancala board. The children could investigate the rules and write instructions.

Exploring Colour and Shape

Starting Points

- Gustav Klimt (1862–1918) was an Austrian painter. He is a good artist to use as a starting point when exploring the theme of colour due to the style of his paintings. Later in his life, Klimt began to paint in a much more imaginative way until eventually his creations were very decorative and had hidden meanings. His most well-known work is *The Kiss* (1907–08). Look closely at a picture of *The Kiss*. Ask the children to consider how the artist began to think about the picture and ask questions such as, 'What did he want to portray?', 'What would be the history of the lovers in the picture?' and 'How did he decide which colours to use?' On the whiteboard, make a list of the vocabulary the children use to describe the picture and their other ideas.

- Using a template in the shape of an artist's palette, ask the children to write about their ideas in one half of the palette and in the other, take an area of colour from the picture and reproduce it using coloured pencils or pastels.

Display

- Cut a copy of *The Kiss* into about 30 sections (you will need one section for each class member). Give each child a section, along with a blank square of white paper. Using a range of media such as paint, craypas and oil pastels, ask them to copy their section in detail on the square. They should try to match the colours as closely as possible.

- Assemble all the squares to recreate a complete picture of *The Kiss*. Part of the challenge is putting the image back together – ask groups of children to help with this large jigsaw puzzle!

- As part of this project, the children could also create their own pictures in the style of Klimt.

- Display the large picture above a display board backed in black paper. Before attaching the children's work to the board, ask them to paint patterns in Klimt's style directly onto the board in gold paint.

Resources

- *The Kiss* by Gustav Klimt (1907–08)
- *Farbstudie Quadrate* (1913), *Several Circles* (1926) and *Colour Study: Squares with Concentric Circles* by Wassily Kandinsky.
- CD: *The Carnival of the Animals* by Saint-Saëns

Further Activities

- Ask the children to write some poetry inspired by *The Kiss*. Look again at the image and share ideas around love, relationships and friendships. The shape of the poem should follow the swirling movements used within the painting.

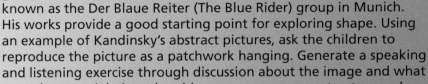

- Wassily Kandinsky (1866–1944) was a Russian-born artist and one of the first creators of pure abstraction in modern painting. He founded the influential group of abstract painters known as the Der Blaue Reiter (The Blue Rider) group in Munich. His works provide a good starting point for exploring shape. Using an example of Kandinsky's abstract pictures, ask the children to reproduce the picture as a patchwork hanging. Generate a speaking and listening exercise through discussion about the image and what materials the children will need to use, for example, material, thread, gold pens, compasses, protractors and so on. Divide a copy of the picture up into sections and give each child or pair a part of the picture and materials. Ask them to produce an interpretation of their section of the picture. Assemble all their sections together to create the hanging. They should then complete a journal, explaining how they felt, what they thought, what they needed during its making. Display the hanging with the children's journals.

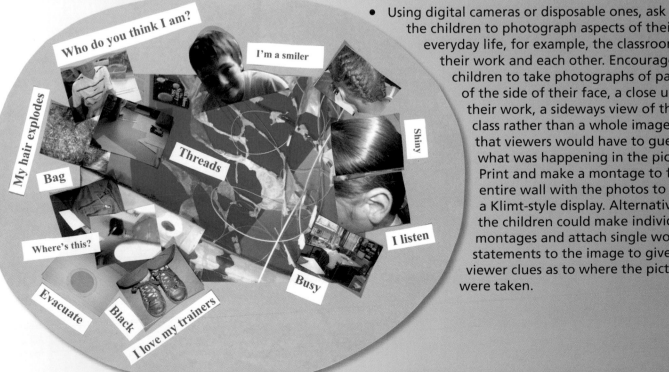

- Using digital cameras or disposable ones, ask the children to photograph aspects of their everyday life, for example, the classroom, their work and each other. Encourage the children to take photographs of parts of the side of their face, a close up of their work, a sideways view of the class rather than a whole image so that viewers would have to guess what was happening in the picture. Print and make a montage to fill an entire wall with the photos to create a Klimt-style display. Alternatively, the children could make individual montages and attach single words or statements to the image to give the viewer clues as to where the pictures were taken.

Maths

- Cut out a series of squares and rectangles in different colours and materials, for example, fabric, tinfoil and so on. Ask the children to identify the properties of the shapes – sides, faces, edges. Place shapes in a tessellating pattern on large pieces of card. For a challenge, restrict the tessellation area or insist that there are five squares and five rectangles within the pattern. Discuss how many sides, edges and faces are in their completed patterns.

- Using an example of Klimt's work, draw a jigsaw template on the reverse side. Cut out the pieces and give to a group of children to complete. Ask the children to list the shapes within the piece of the poster puzzle.

- Using the art activity on page 62, create another picture in the style of Klimt. Ask the children to re-assemble the picture using the different sections. This could be done in small groups as a problem-solving challenge. Extend the activity by counting how many different shapes can be found on the artwork. They should describe the shapes using mathematical language.

- Using 1cm² paper, ask the children to colour a single square. Next, colour in a 2×2 square. Double this to 4×4 and colour this in a different colour. How many squares can they find before they run out of paper? Extend by using this to improve multiplication tables.

- Using the mathematical ideas based on the abstract works of both Klimt and Kandinsky, make a 3-D town out of numbers. Give each child a shoebox or cereal box. Cover the inside of the box with blue paper for sky. Cover the bottom of the lid with green paper for grass. Draw and cut out the numbers 0–11 in different colours. Glue some numbers to the back of the box, but save a few for the front of the display. Draw, cut and glue together houses with doors and windows. Glue the 3-D houses to the lid. Display all the houses together to make an abstract number town.

PE

- Walk around imaginary 2-D shapes in the playground, for example, a circle, a square, a triangle. Extend the task by having groups working together to make 3-D shapes with their bodies.

- Mark the corners of the hall with shape cards (square, triangle, hexagon, circle). Ask the children to run around until you say stop. Give a clue, for example, shape with three sides, four right angles and so on. The children should run to the appropriate corner.

Wassily Kandinsky

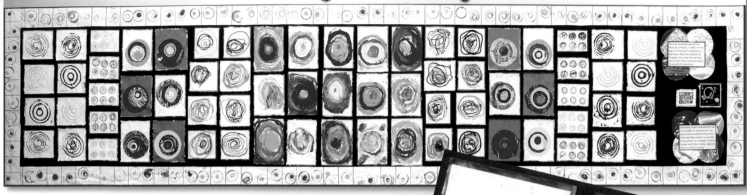

Art

- Create some dream art in the style of Klimt. Ask the children to remember a recent dream they had – what did they see and where did it happen? Ask them to draw dreams on paper. Mount it on card covered in silver foil. Drape strips of shiny bubble wrap from it. As an extension, start a dream journal with the children. Decorate the covers so that it is a special book for writing and drawing their dreams in.

- Cut out a 10cm² piece of card. Cut a square within this measuring 7cm². This becomes an artist's seeing eye. Place this over any piece of art. Ask the children to record on a sheet what they can see. Ask questions such as, 'What colours did you see?', 'What shapes?', 'What patterns?' and 'What did they remind you of?'

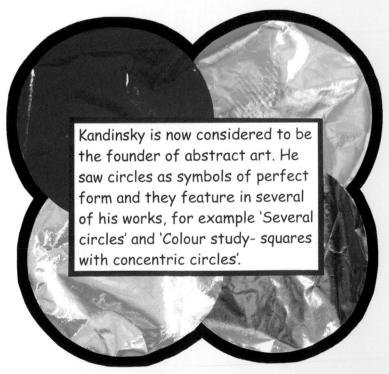

Kandinsky is now considered to be the founder of abstract art. He saw circles as symbols of perfect form and they feature in several of his works, for example 'Several circles' and 'Colour study- squares with concentric circles'.

- Using the circular work of Kandinsky, such as *Farbstudie Quadrate* (1913), produce 3-D sculpture work using wool, shiny paper and card. Mount within a circular shape drawn by the children using wax crayons. The children could label their work by explaining why they used certain materials and how they felt about their artwork once completed.

Music

- Display a large picture of contrasting colours by Kandinsky. Talk about the title of the picture and ask for their responses. For example, examine the title, shapes and colours. Ask the children to choose percussion instruments to represent the colours in the picture. In groups, they should create a piece to reflect the mood of the image.

- Play music from the period of Kandinsky and Klimt, for example, *The Carnival of the Animals* by Saint-Saëns (1835–1921). Listen to the music and ask the children to create a short dance in groups.

Artists

Starting Points

- Show the class Van Gogh's *Room at Arles* (1889). Ask them to comment on what is in the room – bed, chairs, small table. Next, ask them what the picture shows belonging to the artist – clothes hung on a peg, toiletries on the table, pictures on the wall. Ask them what type of person the artist was by looking closely at the colours and objects in the painting.

- Once they have thoroughly explored the painting, tell them key facts about Vincent van Gogh – he was Dutch, born in the nineteenth century, painted many pieces of art but only managed to sell one during his lifetime. His painting style involved the use of rich bold colours and coarse brushwork.

- Write poems inspired by a Van Gogh landscape, such as *Starry Night* (1889). Look at the image and brainstorm the shapes in the picture on a whiteboard. Collect a vocabulary bank of words, such as 'swirling' and 'circles'. Ask the children to work in pairs to produce a poem using metaphors that reflect the image, for example, the sun swirls like a washing machine.

Resources

- *Room at Arles* (1889), *Starry Night* (1889), *Sunflowers* (1888) and *Self Portrait with Straw Hat* (1887) by Vincent van Gogh.
- *Dora Maar with Cat* (1941), *Self-Portrait with a Palette* (1906), *Self-Portrait* (1907), *Portrait of Ambroise Vollard* (1910), *Rembrandtesque Figure and Cupid* (1969) and *Dove with olive branch* (1949) by Pablo Picasso.
- *East Yorkshire. Spring Landscape* (2004), *A Larger Valley. Millington* (2004) and *Bigger Trees Near Water* (2007) by David Hockney.
- *Atlantic Tree Family* (2004), *First Love, The Hug, From Eden* (2006) and *Flower Power* by Romero Britto.
- www.mrpicassohead.com/create.html
- www.sunflowers.com/commerce/index.php
- www.britto.com

Display

- Take a selection of prints from the work of Van Gogh. Each child should choose a print and reproduce them using different media, for example, craypas or paint mixed with flour.

- Ask the children to write about what they can find in the paintings – trees, stars, a small town. Extend by asking them to write down their reasons for choosing that particular print.

- Mount the paintings and the children's writing and place on a large display board with the artist's name above it.

Further Activities

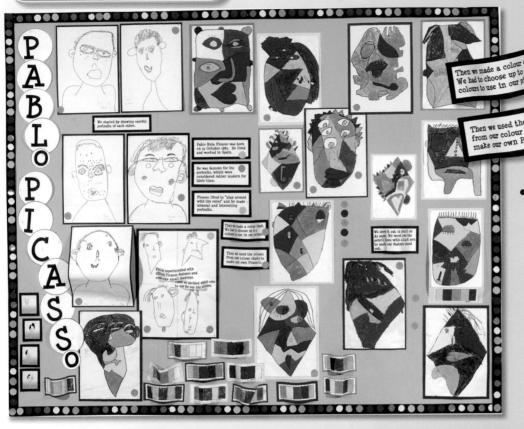

We started by drawing careful portraits of each other.

Pablo Ruiz Picasso was born on 25 October 1881. He lived and worked in Spain.

He was famous for his portraits, which were considered rather modern for their time.

Picasso liked to 'play around with the rules' and he made unusual and interesting portraits.

Then we made a colour chart. We had to choose up to 5 colours to use in our picture.

Then we used the colours from our colour charts to make our own Picassos.

We experimented with different Picasso features and made some small drawings. Then we decided which one to use for our big picture.

We drew it out in pencil on A3 paper. We went over the pencil lines with a black pen to make our features stand out.

- Look at Pablo Picasso's portraits, such as *Dora Maar with Cat* (1941), *Self-Portrait with a Palette* (1906), *Self-Portrait* (1907) and *Portrait of Ambroise Vollard* (1910). Discuss what is different about the style in which these paintings were produced (they are from different periods in his life, they are of different people and the style in which they are painted differs even though the same artist painted them all). Ask the children to sketch a portrait in the style of Picasso. Then they should use colour charts and mix the paint to produce tones. Paint the portraits using these colours. The children should then write labels explaining how they completed the portraits. Mount the portraits and labels to create a display.

- Look at Picasso's *Rembrandtesque Figure and Cupid* (1969). Discuss who the two figures in the painting are. One is a woman who is looking straight at the audience. She dominates the picture, while at her right-hand side is the small figure of Cupid. They are not looking at each other nor do they seem to have any relationship. Ask the children to make up a line of dialogue for each of the characters in the painting that will reveal their feelings. They could write their dialogue in speech bubbles which could then be cut out and displayed next to the copy of the picture.

We drew it out in pencil on A3 paper. We went over the pencil lines with a black pen to make our features stand out.

- Ask the children to imagine that they interviewed an artist and are then to produce a full page newspaper spread.

- Produce a specialised review of an art piece, include an illustration of the work or print off a copy from the Internet.

- Contact local artists and invite them to show and discuss their work in class. Encourage the children to ask questions as part of a speaking and listening exercise.

- Have a selection of images showing artists work available. Use these as a stimulus for discussion based on 'How successful is this work of art?' The children could record their thoughts on paper or the whiteboard. They should give reasons for their thoughts.

- Look at the work of Picasso (1881–1973) in particular, *Dove with olive branch* (1949). Record the children's thoughts about the picture on the whiteboard. Then ask them to write a poem for peace – use the haiku format and display on templates of Picasso's *Dove with olive branch*.

peace is silent and calm. It feels like Harmony Like Laughing, Peaceful. it is so golden sunshine showering it is so joyful. or maybe it is like a dove soaring through the wind actually peace is Heaven or maybe a cherub. By Aria Shahrokhshahi

Cross-curricular Links

Maths

- Access the website www.mrpicassohead.com/create.html and ask the children to create their own Picasso head by selecting features and dropping them into the portrait. The children could then cut and paste their image and transfer it to graph paper. They should count how many squares there are for noses, ears, lips and make a class comparison chart.

Science

- Looking at a collection of pictures of Pablo Picasso, Romero Britto and Vincent van Gogh, ask the children to identify how many primary colours (red, yellow and blue) are mixed to yield secondary colours (orange, green, violet) in the pictures. Make a colour wheel based on their observation.

- Van Gogh painted *Sunflowers* (1888), a still life. The website www.sunflowers.com/commerce/index.php is a gardening guide for growing sunflowers. Grow sunflowers in pots on the windowsill. Have a competition to see whose grows the biggest. Ask the children to write an instructional text for planting seeds and an illustrated set for a child from another country to follow. Produce a graph to monitor how long the seeds take to grow.

- Discuss with the class the fact that Picasso was a child prodigy whose first word was 'piz', short for 'lapiz', the Spanish word for pencil. Both Picasso and Van Gogh changed the way art was produced and had very distinctive styles. Many people feel that the brains of exceptionally talented people are bigger than others! Tell the class that by using newspaper and white tights they are going to create a 3-D sculpture of the 'Brain of an artist'. Place wadded balls of newspaper together and secure using masking tape. Once a large circular ball has been made, use PVA glue and white tissue paper to conceal the masking tape. Then get several pairs of white thick tights. Stuff these with newspaper to create tubes. Drape the tubes at the top of the white ball to resemble the brain. Use the sculpture as a starting point to discuss what things each child is exceptionally good at. It can be something as simple as kicking a football, sharpening pencils really quickly, or more specific, such as knowing your times tables.

Geography

- Look at images of landscapes by various artists, for example, *East Yorkshire. Spring Landscape* (2004), *A Larger Valley. Millington* (2004) and *Bigger Trees Near Water* (2007) by David Hockney (born 1937). Discuss how artists use different techniques to portray the landscapes. Can the children reproduce these techniques in their own pictures of landscapes? Invite the children to create landscapes using pastels and display these with a reference to how they think the artist chose the landscapes and what media he used in his painting.

Art

- Discuss the works of the artist Britto. Like Picasso, he was a child prodigy. Born in Brazil in 1963, he now lives in New York. He is known as the King of Pop Art. His work is full of vibrant colours separated by black bold lines. Besides being an artist, he is very involved with charities such as Amnesty International and the Red Cross. Discuss a range of Britto's work, such as *Atlantic Family Tree* (2004), *First Love, The Hug* and *Flower Power*. Focus on the colours and lines that build up each part of each picture. Ask the children to use crayons, craypas and wax resist to build up the pictures. Display their pictures next to information about the work of the artist which can be found on his official website www.britto.com.

- Display a copy of the picture *Self Portrait with Straw Hat* (1887) by Van Gogh. Ask the children to pretend they are the artist. What kind of a day would they have had when this picture was painted? How did they feel? Why would they be wearing a straw hat? Ask them to draw their own self portraits to reflect their mood that day. Describing their mood may help them to focus on what to include in the picture.

Design and Technology

- Using plasticine or salt dough, make a 3-D copy of a Britto work, for example, *From Eden* (2006), which is a snake with an apple on its head. Link the sculpture with the story of Adam and Eve in the Bible. Why is the snake smiling? Does it have the apple on its head for a reason?

- Using wadded newspaper and masking tape, make a large portrait head shape. Cover completely with masking tape. Cut out the corner edge of a cereal box and attach it to the face with masking tape to make a nose. Repeat the process to make a chin that juts out. Place strips of newspaper to create eyes and secure all these added features with masking tape. Use pieces of card to make the hair/headdress. Cover the shape by using PVA glue and brown or cream tissue paper so none of the masking tape is showing. Once the shape is covered, spray it with gold metallic paint.

My Locality

Resources
- www.earth.google.com
- www.timeanddate.com/worldclock

- Compare your local area to another locality. In this example, the children compared Nottingham and Skegness. Talk about the fact that Nottingham is an inland city whereas Skegness is on the coast. Lots of families travel from Nottingham to Skegness for weekends or day trips. Ask the children to research their local area and compare it with one they travel to on holiday regularly. Contact the local tourist industry to send the class pamphlets about your area. Use these to divide your locality into areas such as tourism, shopping, local attractions such as parks or theme parks, transport and so on. Give a small group of children one of these topics each and ask them to research it in depth. Ask them to suggest people who could come into school to explain more about their topic, such as a member of the community who owns a shop or a member of a leisure centre who would explain what activities are available for children.

Display

- Mount two display boards – one to feature your locality and the other a contrasting one, such as Nottingham and Skegness.

- Print out main landmarks for each locality, such as the beach in Skegness. Have a selection of pictures available to give to the class.

- Ask the children to draw their own version of the landmark using chalks. Mount and display on boards together with the original pictures.

- Cut out a large letter which is the first letter of your town or city. Children write down any things they like or know about their locality. Stick the writing and pictures down on the large letters and display.

- Make pamphlets from A4 paper about your locality.

- Using the Internet, print off maps of your immediate locality such as your school, the town it is in and finally the area, such as Nottinghamshire. Do the same with the contrasting locality.

Further Activities

- Discuss why many people live in some areas, and very few, or none in others. Compare the population size in your local area to other areas near where you live.

- Discuss why so many people want to live somewhere else. Mark onto a map where the children live at the moment and where they might like to live in the future. Write down reasons and then ask them to research that place using the Internet.

- Take a series of photographs of your locality and enlarge them. Use these as story starters, for example, a picture of a castle on top of the hill may inspire: 'The men swarmed up the side of the hill. You could hear their anger in their voices.'

- Look at the history of our locality and choose key events that the children will research and turn into newspaper reports. Mount the research with the newspaper headlines and either historical photographs or original newspaper articles, and copies of the photographs the children have reproduced in a range of art materials.

- Record locality-themed work in a book made out of two pieces of sturdy card (or the inside of cereal packets). Place several sheets of A4 card or paper in between the covers and staple together. Decorate the cover by tearing tissue paper to create a feature of your locality.

Cross-curricular Links

Geography

- Use the website www.earth.google.com to find your school and its locality using satellite pictures (children may want to find their homes as well). Ask the children to identify features of their area – parks, shops, back gardens, playing fields and so on. Create an aerial collage of your local area using a variety of materials.

An aerial collage

Art

- Choose an artist local to your area. In this example, the children chose L.S.Lowry (Laurence Stephen Lowry 1887–1976). Using the work of the artist as a starting point, give the children examples of his work and ask them to reproduce a group picture in the same style using the same media.

- Create a photo montage of a part of your local area. During a class visit to the area, take a number of photographs and attach them together to create one large landscape on a display board. Add detail to the picture depending on the area. In this example, the children painted poppies to stick on the landscape after visiting a meadow in the area.

Design and Technology

- Take a major landmark from your local area and research its history, for example, a castle or sculpture. Using card, junk material and papier mâché, make a 3-D model of the landmark. The example shown in the middle of the display above is a statue of a soldier that stands in the main square.

Maths

- Using the website www.timeanddate.com/worldclock, identify the differences between your locality and the classrooms around the world. Extend by finding out what time they go to bed, get up and go to school.